ENHANCING PRODUCTION

A Research and Case Based Approach

ENHANCING PRODUCTION

A Research and Case Based Approach

Abhinav Chauhan
Sanjeev Bansal
Ajay Rana

I.K. International Publishing House Pvt. Ltd.
NEW DELHI

Published by
I.K. International Publishing House Pvt. Ltd.
S-25, Green Park Extension
Uphaar Cinema Market
New Delhi–110 016 (India)
E-mail:info@ikinternational.com
Website: www.ikbooks.com

ISBN: 978-93-84588-33-5

Published by Krishan Makhijani for I.K. International Publishing House Pvt. Ltd., S-25, Green Park Extension, Uphaar Cinema Market, New Delhi–110 016 and Printed by Rekha Printers Pvt. Ltd., Okhla Industrial Area, Phase II, New Delhi–110 020.

FOREWORD

This book, "**Enhancing Production**" is a unique work done by three highly qualified writers, who bring a rare combination of great knowledge and vast experience in the area of management, in the area of engineering as well as in the area of combination of both.

Dr. Abhinav Chauhan is an extraordinarily competent engineer with the acumen and talent in production technologies, which can rarely have a match. He has shared his experiences and observations in the production units overseas as well as in India and most importantly own big production unit, which is regarded in the country as one of the best production plants in the country.

The book most successfully tackles the versatile area of production engineering, system engineering, software engineering and integrated product and process development.

Statistical product control for software empirical analysis of massive maintenance process, modern statistical control and improvements, the ways and means to improve performance, new patterns of management, the human side of enterprise, troubleshooting and solutions of occurring problems in production processes and the most analytical and strategic way of product development have been expressed in most pragmatic way on the basis of own experiences.

The methods and ways to reduce the production cost and to make the production with high quality standards, based on own experiences have been depicted in a way that everyone can learn from that.

The co-writers of this book, Dr. Sanjeev Bansal and Dr. Ajay Rana have given their valuable inputs, having their industry and corporate world experiences and also the experiences gained through teaching and training a very large number of students in the domain of management and engineering.

This book is of immense value for all the students of engineering and management, as well as for the faculty members and also for all those who are managing and working in the production in industrial units. This would provide them new insight and equip them with the solutions to cope with all challenges in manufacturing sector.

Ashok K. Chauhan

(Dr. Ashok K. Chauhan)
Founder President, Ritnand Balved Education Foundation (RBEF)
(The Foundation of Amity Institutions & Sponsoring Body of Amity Universities) &
Chairman, AKC Group of Companies

PREFACE

Production is a process of combining various material inputs and various other inputs (plans, strategies, knowhow and meticulous planning) in order to make something for consumption (the output). It is the act of creating output, a good or service, which has value and contributes to the utility of individuals.

Economic development is created in a production process, meaning all economic activities that aim directly or indirectly to satisfy human needs. The degree to which the needs are satisfied is often accepted as a measure of economic wellbeing. The satisfaction of needs originates from the use of the commodities which are produced. The need satisfaction increases when the quality-price-ratio of the commodities improves and more satisfaction is achieved at less cost. Improving the quality-price-ratio of commodities is to a producer, an essential method to enhance the production performance, but this kind of gains distributed to customers cannot be measured with production data.

In recent years, quality manufacturing is growing in an exponential way. The quality of manufacturing plays a very important role in the success or failure in a manufacturing unit. Thus, units measure their performance in terms of quality and reliability of the manufactured products. For this purpose, manufacturing should follow quality models, guidelines, six sigma, employee technical skills, principles of physics as well as innovation. The perception of employees is also important for quality output. Another important factor is the teamwork. The teamwork is directly related to the work culture of the manufacturing unit(s). The demand of the customer is ever increasing – the quality of products that we expect is increasing day by day. The cost, we are willing to pay, is always lesser than what was earlier.

What does manufacturing industries do in this socio-economic scenario? They bring the cost of manufacturing down. It is a well-known fact that any activity not adding value is an unwanted activity. Thus, one has to look at the process carefully and eliminate these. The other areas which will help in reducing cost of modern manufacturing units are proper applications of principles related to the processes and innovation.

This book is an attempt to discuss about the above-mentioned areas and their effectiveness in enhancing production at reduced costs, with special reference to mould manufacturing and plastic moulding industry.

Abhinav Chauhan
Sanjeev Bansal
Ajay Rana

ACKNOWLEDGEMENTS

This book is the result of the advice, guidance and sharing of the valuable experiences and observations from worthy mentors, industrial and corporate partners and the sacrifice of our family members. It is our privilege that now we have the opportunity to express our gratitude to each one of them.

Our deepest and sincere gratefulness goes to the Great Almighty for inspiring us to come out with this book, which is the result of our sincere efforts and research of four years.

We extend our wholehearted submission to Dr. Ashok K. Chauhan, Founder President, Amity Universe, who is the guiding force behind this research and ultimately this book, and all our achievements are dedicated to him.

It is the most sincere sacrifice from dear Palak that she even at late hours, while I was writing the book, said, "Abhinav, your book is going to be a masterpiece," which encouraged me tremendously. The cooperation from dear Sonia providing peaceful atmosphere and controlling the whole household affairs herself to give a conducive environment to concentrate on the deep intellectual work and saying, "Sanjeev, you are writing a book which would become a unique publication" and also the all-time inspiration and care taken by Madhvi and saying from time to time, "Ajay, I am confident that your book would greatly help in the mission of the Hon'ble Prime Minister - Make in India." This book would not have come to the light of the day, without such inspiration, motivation and cooperation from them.

This book is an example of a great teamwork, where all of us have worked within our defined roles and have brought contribution as a whole.

Abhinav Chauhan
Sanjeev Bansal
Ajay Rana

THE AUTHORS

The first author, **Dr. Abhinav Chauhan** has an innate passion to make use of information technology as a tool for cost-effective measures in manufacturing process. Dr. Chauhan has worked tirelessly to bring sea changes in the production facilities of various companies.

About 15 years back, when Abhinav was a young person of 22 years, the Founder President of AMITY Universities and Educational Institutions as well as Chairman of AKC Group of Companies recognized Dr. Chauhan's aptitude in research and innovation in production and guided him for his higher studies in UK where he completed his M. Sc in Manufacturing, Management and Information Systems from University of the West of England, Bristol. His education has always been focused upon manufacturing and product development. He did a course on product development from M.I.T., U.S.A; M.B.A in International Business and Production form AMITY University, Noida, and also completed his Ph. D with the thesis *A Framework for Evaluating Optimization of Manufacturing Techniques* from AMITY University.

Dr. Chauhan's revolutionary innovative works have been acknowledged by industry veterans and entrepreneurs from an arena of industries, in India and abroad, who rely on Kunstocom (one of the companies of the AKC Group), for benchmarking.

Dr. Chauhan has introduced many new technologies developed by him in production lines of home appliances.

Dr. Chauhan has an inherent aptitude for scientific temperament and several of his articles have been published in renowned scientific journals. He has 20 patents to his credit out of which he has already successfully commercialized 3 patents.

Dr. Chauhan has aplenty human values inbuilt in him. He commands great respect, love and affection among his colleagues, seniors and juniors alike. His extraordinary helping nature unfolds a nurturing environment for each one of them.

Dr. Chauhan relaxes drawing illustrations, most of which are framed and mounted at his workplace. These hand-made artworks reflect his self-driven nature to complete projects with finesse – whether it's racing horses or the beauty of a human form. He loves spending his free time with the family.

Dr Sanjeev Bansal is the Director and Head of Amity Business School (ABS). Under his leadership, ABS has scaled heights and has been ranked in the top ten Business Schools of India consistently. ABS also has recently been confereed with prestigious "Palmer Award" by Wharton University, Pennsylvania.

An admired academician, his doctoral work is an exemplary study in the area of decision sciences from Delhi. In an acclaimed career span of about 24 years in teaching, research and consultancy, he has been invited to be a part of several prestigious academic/professional bodies, and in his advisory capacity he has steered them to success.

He is an avid researcher and has more than 95 research papers in prestigious journals to his credit. He has authored six books which have been exceptionally well received internationally. He has guided several research scholars to produce works of immense educational impact.

Apart from his areas of specialization, he also likes to explore and research the vistas of spirituality, management and quality of work life.

During his distinguished career he has had many accomplishments and is hailed as an institution builder, a loved teacher and an ardent researcher.

Dr Ajay Rana is Founder Director/Professor/ Mentor of more than 27 different departments and innovative programs at the Amity Grou. He has a rich experience in the industry and academia for more than 15 years. Dr Rana has had an outstanding academic record and he has been a product of prestigious systems throughout. He obtained his Ph.D. in Computer Science and Engineering and Master of Technology (M.Tech) in Computer Science and Engineering. He has visited many of the worlds' prestigious universities for Education & Research (E&R) Oriented Projects.

He has published more than 177 Research Papers in reputed journals and proceedings of international and national conferences. He has co-authored five books and co-edited 36 conference proceedings. He has delivered invited lectures in more than 36 technical and management workshop/conference programs in India and abroad. He has undertaken 18 sponsored research projects and 9 major systems based Management/HRD consultancies in a number of reputed organizations both public and private, in India and abroad.

Dr Rana has received a number of awards and honors like the eduCLUSION AWARD 2014, for displaying extraordinary initiative in expanding the Private Institutional space for Higher Technical Education by India Engineering Watch (Singapore, 2014), Italian Machine Tool Technology Award (IMTTA) in Italy (2014), International WHO'S WHO of Professionals, Washington USA. (2014) , IT Next CIO Award 2011 in Pune, Best Advisor SIFE at Mumbai in 2011, etc., and was a recipient of the National Merit Scholarship.

His tenure has led to an overall excellence in education, research, infrastructure and systemic development of organization. His current focus is to enhance the Quality of Education through Strategic Quality Initiatives.

CONTENTS

1

INTRODUCTION

SIGNIFICANCE OF MANUFACTURING

The 'Make in India' initiative taken by Prime Minister Mr Narendra Modi promises to put India's manufacturing sector into the world map as a manufacturing hub. With a modest 16% contribution to the GDP currently, the Indian manufacturing is pitched to contribute 25% to its GDP in relative terms. This will mean that manufacturing will be the second most important sector, after the services sector. This will lead to creation of more enterprises, jobs and products for trading and consumption in the global manufacturing market. Globally, India is positioned second to China in terms of competitiveness, but all that is set to change and the scale will perhaps tilt in India's favour soon. A recent report says Foxconn, a Taiwanese manufacturing group and Apple's largest global manufacturing partner, is planning to invest hugely in India creating one million jobs alone by 2020. This is because of rising labor cost and lower investor confidence in China, according to the same report.

The Advanced Manufacturing Partnership offers one glimpse into the future of manufacturing. The group, created by the US President Mr Barack Obama, has identified eleven areas of technology that it believes will play a crucial role in determining competitiveness in manufacturing—and that it believes should be the focus of national R&D efforts. Enterprises and entrepreneurs will have to constantly adapt to the changes which will come thick and fast. Enhancing productivity will always remain a key challenge. The boundaries will always need to be pushed. New formulae will have to be arrived at. Before we go further in the direction of creating a framework for enhancing productivity, let us refresh ourselves with the basic concepts which will be applied and referred to later.

PRODUCTION CONCEPT

Production is a process of combining various material inputs and immaterial inputs (plans, knowhow etc.) in order to make something for consumption (output). It is the act of creating output, a good or service which has value and contributes to the utility of individuals. Economic well-being is created in a production process, which encompasses all economic activities that aim directly or indirectly to satisfy human needs. The degree to which the needs are satisfied is often accepted as a measure of economic well-being. The satisfaction of needs originates from the use of the commodities which are produced. The need satisfaction increases when the quality-price-ratio of the commodities improves and more satisfaction is achieved at a lesser cost. Improving the quality-price-ratio of commodities is an essential way for a producer to enhance the production performance, but this kind of gain extended to customers cannot be measured with production data.

Economic well-being also improves due to the growth of incomes that are gained from growing and efficient production. The most important forms of production are:

- Market production,
- Public production and
- Production in households.

In order to understand the origin of the economic well-being, we must understand the above-mentioned three production processes. All of them have production functions of their own which interact with each other. Market production is the prime source of economic well-being and is therefore the 'primus motor' of the modern economy. Note that when we later discuss production, we will refer to market production. When we discuss a single unit in the production process, the term 'company' is used.

Production as a source of economic well-being

In principle there are two main activities in an economy – production and consumption. Similarly there are two kinds of actors – producers and consumers. Economic well-being is made possible by efficient production and by the interaction between producers and consumers. In the interaction process, consumers can be identified with two roles, both of which generate well-being. Consumers can be both customers of the producers and suppliers to the producers. The customers' well-being arises from the commodities which they are buying and the suppliers' well-being is related to the income which they receive as compensation for the production inputs they have delivered to the producers.

Stakeholders of Production

The stakeholders of production are persons, groups or organizations with an interest in a producing company. Economic well-being originates in efficient production and it is distributed through the interaction among the company's stakeholders. The stakeholders of companies are economic factors which have an economic interest in the company. Based on the similarities of their interests, stakeholders can be classified into three groups in order to differentiate their interests and mutual relations. The three groups are as follows:

- Customers
- Suppliers
- Producers.

The interests of these stakeholders and their relations to companies are described briefly below. Our purpose here is to establish a framework for further analysis.

Customers

The customers of a company are typically consumers, other market producers, or producers in the public sector. Each of them has their individual production functions. Due to competition, the price-quality-ratios of commodities tend to improve and this brings the benefits of better productivity to the customers. The customers get more for less. In households and the public sector, this means that more need satisfaction is achieved at a lesser cost. For this reason, the productivity of customers can increase over time even though their incomes can remain unchanged.

Suppliers

The suppliers of companies are typically producers of materials, energy, capital and services. They all have their individual production functions. The changes in prices or qualities of supplied commodities have an effect on both the actors' (company and suppliers) production functions. We come to the conclusion that the production functions of the company and its suppliers are in a state of continuous change.

Producers

The incomes are generated for those participating in production, i.e., the labour force, the society and the owners. These stakeholders are referred to here as producer communities or, in a more precise form, as producers. The producer communities have a common interest in maximizing their incomes. These parties which contribute to production receive increased incomes from the growing and developing production.

The well-being gained through commodities stems from the price-quality relations of the commodities. Due to competition and ever-changing developments in the marketplace, the price-quality relations of commodities tend to improve over time. Typically, the quality of a commodity goes up and the price goes down over time. This development favorably affects the production functions of customers. Customers get more for less. Customers get more satisfaction at a lesser cost. This type of well-being generation can only partially be calculated from the production data. This situation is presented in this study. The producer community (labour force, society and owners) earns income as compensation for the inputs they deliver to production. When the production grows and becomes more efficient, the income tends to increase. In production, this brings about an increased ability to pay salaries, taxes and profits. The growth of production and improved productivity generates additional income for the producing community. Similarly, the high income level achieved in the community is a result of the high volume of production and its high level of performance. This type of well-being generation – as mentioned earlier – can be reliably calculated from the production data.

MAIN PROCESSES OF A MANUFACTURING COMPANY

A producing company can be divided into sub-processes in different ways. The following five are identified as the main processes, each with a logic, objectives, theories and key figures of its own. It is important to examine each of them individually – as a part of the whole – in order to be able to measure and understand them. The main processes of a company are as follows:

- Real process
- Income distribution process
- Production process
- Monetary process
- Market value process

The production output is created in the real process. Gains of production are distributed in the income distribution process and these two processes constitute the production process. The production process and its sub-processes, the real process and income distribution process, occur simultaneously, and only the production process is identifiable and measurable by the traditional accounting practices. The real process and income distribution process can be identified and measured by extra calculation, and this is why these need to be analyzed separately in order to understand the logic of production and its performance.

A real process generates the production output from the input, and it can be described by means of the production function. It refers to a series of events in production in which the production inputs of different qualities and quantities are combined into products of different qualities and quantities. Products can be physical goods, immaterial services, and most often combinations of both.

The characteristics created into the product by the producer imply surplus value to the consumer, and on the basis of the market price this value is shared by the consumer and the producer in the marketplace. This is the mechanism through which surplus value originates to the consumer and the producer likewise. It is worth noting that surplus values to customers cannot be measured from any production data. Instead the surplus value to a producer can be measured. It can be expressed both in terms of nominal and real values. The real surplus value to the producer is an outcome of the real process, real income, and measured proportionally it means productivity.

Income distribution process of production refers to a series of events in which the unit prices of constant-quality products and inputs alter causing a change in the income distribution among those participating in the exchange. The magnitude of the change in income distribution is directly proportionate to the changes in price of the output and inputs and to their quantities. Productivity gains are distributed, for example, to customers as a lower product selling prices or to the staff as a higher income pay.

The production process consists of the real process and the income distribution process. A result and a criterion of success of the owner is profitability. The profitability of production is the share of the real process result which the owner has been able to keep to himself or herself in the income distribution process. Factors describing the production process are the components of profitability, i.e., returns and costs. They differ from the factors of the real process in that the components of profitability are given at nominal prices, whereas in the real process, the factors are at periodically fixed prices.

The monetary process refers to events related to financing the business. The market value process refers to a series of events in which investors determine the market value of a company in the investment markets.

PRODUCTION GROWTH AND PERFORMANCE

Production growth is often defined as a production increase of an output of a production process. It is usually expressed as a growth percentage depicting the growth of the real production output. The real output is the real value of products produced in a production process and when we subtract the real input from the real output we get the real income. The real output and the real income are generated by the real process of production from the real inputs.

The real process can be described by means of the production function. The production function is a graphical or mathematical expression showing the relationship between the inputs used in production and the outputs achieved. Both graphical and mathematical expressions are presented and demonstrated. The production function is a simple description of the mechanism of income generation in the production process. It consists of two components. These two components are (i) a change in production input and (ii) a change in productivity.

In the case of a single production process, the output is defined as an economic value of products and services produced in the process. When we want to examine an entity of many production processes we have to sum up the value-added created in the single individual processes. This is done in order to avoid the double accounting of intermediate inputs. Value-added is obtained by subtracting the intermediate inputs from the outputs. The most well-known and used measure of value-added is Gross Domestic Product (GDP). It is widely used as a measure of the economic growth of nations and industries.

The growth of production output does not reveal anything about the performance of the production process. The performance of production measures the production's ability to generate income. Because the income from production is generated through a real process, we call it the real income. Similarly, as the production function is an expression of the real process, we could also call it 'income generated by the production function'.

The real income generation follows the logic of the production function. We can distinguish two components in an income change – the income growth caused by an increase in the production input (production volume) and the income growth caused by an increase in productivity. The income growth caused by an increased production volume is determined by moving along the production function graph. The income growth corresponding to a shift of the production function is generated by an increase in productivity. The change of real income signifies a move from one point to the other on the production function. When we want to maximize the production performance, we will have to maximize the income generated by the production function.

The production performance can be measured as an average or an absolute income. Expressing performance both in average (avg) and absolute (abs) quantities is helpful for understanding the welfare effects of production. For measurement of the average production performance, we compute the known productivity ratio:

REAL OUTPUT/REAL INPUT

The absolute income of a performance is obtained by subtracting the real input from the real output as follows:

Real income (abs) = Real output – Real input

The growth of the real income is the increase of the economic value which can be distributed between the production stakeholders. With the aid of the production model, we can perform the average and absolute accounting in one calculation. Maximizing the production performance requires use of the absolute measure, i.e., the real income and its derivatives as a criterion of production performance. The differences between the absolute and average performance measures can be illustrated with the help of relationship of marginal and average productivity. The maximum for the production performance is achieved at the volume where the marginal productivity is zero. The maximum for the production performance is the maximum of the real incomes. In practice, decisions are made in a limited range of the production functions, but the principle is still the same – the maximum real income is aimed at. An important conclusion can be drawn. When we try to maximize the welfare effects of production, we have to maximize the real income formation. Maximizing productivity leads to a suboptimum, i.e., to losses of incomes.

PRODUCTION MODEL

A production model is a numerical description of the production process and is based on the prices and the quantities of inputs and outputs. There are two main approaches to operationalize the concept of production function. We can use mathematical formulae, which are typically used in macroeconomics (in growth accounting) or arithmetic models, which are typically used in microeconomics and management accounting. We do not present the former approach here, but refer to the survey *Growth Accounting* by Hulten. We use here arithmetical models because they are like the models of management accounting, illustrative and easily understood and applied in practice. Furthermore, they are integrated to management accounting, which is a practical advantage. A major advantage of the arithmetical model is its capability to the depict production function as a part of the production process. Consequently, the production function can be understood, measured, and examined as a part of production process. There are different production models according to different interests. Here, we use a production income model and a production analysis model in order to demonstrate production function as a phenomenon and a measureable quantity.

In this context, we define the quality requirements for the production data used in productivity accounting. The most important criterion of good measurement is the homogeneity of the measurement object. If the object is not homogenous, then the measurement result may include changes in both quantity and quality, but their respective shares will remain unclear. In productivity accounting, this criterion requires that every item of output and input must appear in accounting as homogenous. In other words, the inputs and the outputs are not allowed to be aggregated in measuring and accounting. If they are aggregated, they are no longer homogenous and hence the measurement results may be biased. Both, the absolute and relative surplus value, have been calculated in the example. Absolute value is the difference of the output and input values and the relative value is their relation, respectively. The surplus value calculation in the example is at a nominal price, calculated at the market price of each period.

PRODUCTION ANALYSIS MODEL

The model used here is a typical production analysis model by help of which it is possible to calculate the outcome of the real process, income distribution process and production process. The starting point is a profitability calculation using surplus value as a criterion of profitability. The surplus value calculation is the only valid measure for understanding the connection between profitability and productivity or understanding the connection between real process and production process. A valid measurement of total productivity necessitates considering all production inputs, and the surplus value calculation is the only calculation to conform to the requirement. If we omit an input in productivity or income accounting, this means that the omitted input can be used unlimitedly in production without any impact on the accounting results.

Accounting and interpreting

The process of calculating is best understood by applying the term *ceteris paribus*, i.e. 'all other things being the same', stating that at a time only the impact of one changing factor be introduced to the phenomenon being examined. Therefore, the calculation can be presented as a process, advancing step by step. First, the impacts of the income distribution process, and then, the impacts of the real process on the profitability of the production, are calculated. The first step of the calculation is to separate the impacts of the real process and the income distribution process, respectively, from the change in profitability.

The production is on the side of 'increasing returns' on the production function, when

- The productivity and production volume increase or
- The productivity and production volume decrease

The production is on the side of 'diminishing returns' on the production function, when

- The productivity decreases and volume increases or
- The productivity increases and volume decreases

Production engineering is a combination of manufacturing technology with management science. A production engineer typically has a wide knowledge of engineering practices and is aware of the management challenges related to production. The goal is to accomplish the production process in the smoothest, most judicious and most economical way. Production engineering encompasses the application of castings, machining processing, joining processes, metal cutting and tool design, metrology, machine tools, machining systems, automation, jigs and fixtures, die and mould design and material science, design of automobile parts, and machine designing and manufacturing. Production engineering also overlaps substantially with manufacturing engineering and industrial engineering.

In industry, once the design is realized, production engineering concepts regarding work-study, ergonomics, operation research, manufacturing management, materials management, production planning, etc., play important roles in efficient production processes. These deal with integrated design and efficient planning of the entire manufacturing system, which is becoming increasingly complex with the emergence of sophisticated production methods and control systems.

As we will build a working model for enhancing productivity with reference to an Indian enterprise from the plastic industry, let us, at this point, take a tour of the Indian plastic industry and assess the manufacturing techniques deployed for creating solutions for customers by the industry players.

PLASTIC INDUSTRY

Overview

Ever since 1957, the plastic industry in India has made significant achievements as it made a modest but promising beginning by commencing production of Polystyrene. The chronology of manufacture of Indian polymers is given below:

- Polystyrene, 1957
- Low Density Polyethylene (LDPE), 1959
- Polyvinyl Chloride (PVC), 1961
- High Density Polyethylene (HDPE), 1968
- Polypropylene, 1978

Such a potential Indian market has motivated the entrepreneurs in the country to acquire technical expertise, achieve high quality standards and build capacities in various facets of the booming plastic industry. The phenomenal developments in the plastic machinery sector are coupled with the developments in the petrochemical sector, both of which support the plastic processing sector. This has facilitated the plastic processors to build capacities for servicing the domestic and the overseas markets. Today, the Indian plastic processing sector comprises over 30,000 units which are involved in producing a variety of items through injection moulding, blow moulding, extrusion and calendaring. The capacities built in most segments of this industry coupled with inherent capabilities have made us capable of servicing the overseas markets. The Indian plastic industry has taken great strides and in the past few decades. In fact, the industry has grown to the status of a leading sector in the country with a sizable base.

Plastic material is gaining notable importance in different spheres of activity. The per capita consumption is increasing at a fast pace. Continuous advancements and developments in plastic technology, processing machineries, expertise, and cost-effective manufacturing are fast replacing the typical traditionally used materials. On the basis of value-added share, the Indian plastic industry is about 0.5% of India's Gross Domestic Product (GDP). The export of plastic products also yields about 1% of the country's exports. This sector has a large presence of small scale companies in the industry, which accounts for more than 50% turnover of the industry and provides employment to an estimated 0.4 million people in the country. Approximately, Rs.100 billion has been invested in the form of fixed assets in the plastic processing industry.

With a population over one billion where 40% are under the age of 15 years, opportunities for plastic producers in India include near-term rapid growth in the nation's internal consumption of plastic products. The Indian middle class is 300 million strong and is rising. The annual GDP growth rate is 8%. Typically, in an emerging market, demand growth for plastics is 2 to 2.5 times the GDP growth. Sadly, this is not the case in India where the growth at times has been lower than the GDP growth. The per capita consumption of plastics in India is at 5 kg, which is much lower than that of China which averages 25 kg. But India could very soon see improvement in the production and consumption of plastic. India, today, represents a range of highly promising opportunities for growth of plastic producers worldwide. The fragmented plastic industry in India is beginning to consolidate, governmental regulations and trade barriers are coming down due to India's recent admission to the WTO, and some large North American plastic manufacturers have already begun doing business here. Today, in India there are about 22000 plastic processing units and 150 plastic processing machinery manufactures. The machinery units supply over 2500 machineries per annum. In 1982, the All India Plastic Industries Association (AIPIA) was incorporated to solve various issues related to the import duty of polymers.

Exhibit 1 Indian Plastic Industry at a Glance

Size of the Industry	Today in India there are about 22,000 plastic processing units and 150 plastic processing machinery manufacturers.
Percentage in World Market	In the year 2006, the value of world plastic export was US$ 375 billion and the share of India was less than 1% with exports of worth US$ 3.187 billion.
Market Capitalization	The per capita consumption of plastic products in India is growing and is moving towards 8% GDP growth.

Exhibit 2 Role of Plastic Industry in the Indian Economy

	2005	2015
@ 15% CARG, Consumption of Plastic Polymers	4.7 Million Tonnes	18.9 Million Tonnes
Employment In Plastic Industry (Direct + Indirect)	2.5 Million	9.5 Million
Plastic Industry's Turnover	Rs. 35,000 Crores	Rs. 1,33,245 Crores
Export of Plastic Products @ 30% CARG	US$ 1,900 Millions	US $ 10,215 Millions
Contribution of Polymers and Plastic Products to the Exchequer	Rs. 6,200 Crores	Rs. 15,990 Crores

In the year 2006, the value of world plastic export was US$ 375 billion and the share of India was less than 1%, with exports of worth US$ 3.187 billion. During this same period, the percentage of growth in export was 21%. During this trend of growth in exports, the exports of plastic raw material increased from 55% to 60% of the total export of plastic goods, while the export of processed plastic goods saw a negative growth from 45% to 9%. According to recent reports and analyzes, the industry is said to be losing an opportunity of US$ 300 million through value addition on the raw materials that are exported. The Indian plastic industry today symbolizes a promising industry and, at the same time, has been creating new employment opportunities for people in the country. The per capita consumption of plastic products in India is growing and is moving towards 8% GDP growth. It is at the verge of a high growth rate of over 10%-12% which is contributed by high growth rates, in turn, from the end-user industries. This trend has mainly been driving the automotive sector, since the economy is already showing signs of recovery from the downturn.

- As the plastic industry is heavily dependent on the automotive sector, launching of new cars in the small car segments are expected to drive the demand for plastics.
- India is likely to dominate the rest of the world's plastic as the domestic Indian plastic industry expects an investment of nearly US$ 80 billion over the next decade.
- The Indian government has identified the petrochemicals industry as a 'high priority' sector owing to the fact that plastics play an important role in providing the basic necessities for everyday use, while conserving the scarce natural resources.
- Plastic plays a significant role in the key sectors of the economy, including agriculture, water management, automobiles, transportation, construction, telecommunication and electronics, besides defense and aerospace, computers and power transmission.
- As of now, the Indian plastic industry has enormous potential for growth as the polymer use in India is far below the world level. With increasing competition in the global market and the constant drive to improve our living standards, the scope for use of plastics is bound to increase manifold and make the production double in the coming years.

Manufacturing Techniques

Sensing, measurement and process control

Virtually, all advanced manufacturing techniques have one common aspect: they are driven by computers, processing and working with vast amounts of data. That is why, the devices that capture and record data, such as sensors that monitor humidity, GPS trackers that fix location or calipers that measure a material's thickness, are so crucial. Just as these types of devices increasingly help make smart phones really smart, they also enable intelligent, flexible, reliable and highly efficient manufacturing techniques. In a modern factory, sensors not only help guide increasingly nimble machines, but these also provide the information necessary to manage the operation of the factory as a whole. Products can be tracked from inception to the point of delivery and, in some cases, even beyond. The moment anything goes wrong in the process, e.g., when the humidity inside a spray booth isn't optimum for paint, a sensor can detect it and issue an alert to the machine operator or even to the plant manager's cell phone.

Materials design, synthesis and processing

New machines will require new materials, and new materials will enable the creation of entirely new machines. The development of coatings, composites and other materials is being accelerated through advances that break materials down to atomic or molecular level and allow them to be manipulated, virtually without the help of any lengthy laboratory procedures. Borrowing a page from the widely acknowledged success of the Human Genome Initiative, the Department of Energy and other US agencies launched a Materials Genome Initiative in 2011. The goal was to halve the time that it took to identify a new material and bring it to market – a process that currently takes decades. The technology for lithium-ion batteries, for instance, was first conceived by an Exxon employee in the 1970s, but it was not introduced commercially until the 1990s. Part of the effort involves getting the widely dispersed and cloistered researchers in the field to share their ideas and innovations.

Digital manufacturing technologies

Engineers and designers have been using computer-aided modeling tools for years not only to design products, but also to test, modify and improve them digitally, often bypassing costlier and slower physical testing methods. Cloud computing and inexpensive 3D scanners (it is now possible to do a simple 3D scan with an iPhone) are transporting these methods out of sophisticated facilities and into the mainstream where they can be used by entrepreneurs. Autodesk makes a fully operational CAD software program called 123D Design that is free and allows individuals to do things that auto makers once required mainframe computers to accomplish.

Sustainable manufacturing

The goal is a straightforward, if not an easy one: maximize each atom of matter and joule of energy used in production and waste as little as possible. Energy-efficient manufacturing is a major area of focus here. Manufacturing engineers, for instance, talk about the potential for 'lights out' factories that operate continuously in the dark and do not need to be heated or cooled because they are largely run by robots and other machines. Remanufacturing and recycling may also become more important, as smaller, highly automated local factories become more common, and more priority is placed on locally available materials.

Nano manufacturing

A nanometer is one-billionth of a meter, so nano manufacturing means being able to manipulate materials on a molecular and even atomic scale. Nano materials are expected to play a role in the future in production of articles and devices like high-efficiency solar cells and batteries, bio-system-based medical applications such as a sensor inside one's body that could tell his/her doctor that the cancer is gone, and so on. Future generations of electronics and computing devices may also rely heavily on nano manufacturing.

Take for example, tablet computers that bend when one sits on them, or a piece of wired clothing for conditioning temperature based on body temperature of the person wearing it. Already working their way into the mainstream, these flexible technologies are expected to define the next generation of consumer and computing devices, and are expected to be among the fastest-growing product categories over the next decade. But they require highly advanced manufacturing processes.

Bio manufacturing uses a biological organism, or a part of one, in an artificial manner, to produce a product—like developing drugs and medical compounds. Bio manufacturing has applications in a wide range of areas, including improvements in energy efficiency and in the creation of new methods of nano manufacturing.

Additive manufacturing

Additive manufacturing, popularly known as 3D printing, has become the standard bearer of the next industrial revolution. It is clearly different, it is already available to both professionals and hobbyists, and it is sexy in a geeky, 'Star Trek' sort of way. An item is made, layer by thin layer, until it appears almost magically from seeming thin air. Remember the replicator aboard the starship Enterprise? Yet additive manufacturing is just one of a number of emerging technologies that are likely to produce major changes in the way many things are made in the years to come. Additive manufacturing is not limited to 3D printing alone. One still-emerging process, called cold spraying, involves blasting metallic particles through a nozzle at such high speeds that they bind to each other to form shapes. By precisely controlling the nozzle, machine operators can build up a three-dimensional metal object like a gear much the same way a 3D printer does. It is as though the object as been painted into existence, and it can be done with even exotic metals like titanium.

Three dimensional printers not only hold the promise of achieving high quality at volumes as low as a single unit, but also of opening the door to entirely new designs and material structures and combinations. Printers have been developed that can print over 1,000 materials, including hard plastic, flexible plastic, ceramics and metals. A German manufacturer has developed a process that deposits layers of wood pulp. A San Diego based company, Organovo, is 3D printing human tissue for use in labs. Some printers can now layer more than one material and can enable smart components to be fabricated with embedded sensors and circuitry, such as hearing aids or motion-sensing gloves. There is something interesting in the market – the Replicator. It is a system made by Cybaman Technologies, a British firm, that starts by layering a basic shape and then machines the rough object into its final precise and polished form.

Industrial robots can operate 24 hours a day, seven days a week, with repeated and increasingly fine precision—to hundredths of a second and in less space than is detectable by the human eye. They report accurately on their progress, improve when their performance is tested for efficiency, and become more dexterous when they are fitted with advanced sensor systems. Also, they rarely complain. As robots become ever more widespread, they are becoming more economical too. The expense associated with industrial robots has fallen by as much as 50% compared with human labor since 1990, according to a report by the McKinsey Global Institute. And, with advances in biotechnology and nanotechology, robots are expected to become capable of doing ever more intricate things, like drug processing and growing full-blown human organs.

Advanced forming and joining technologies

Most current mechanical manufacturing processes continue to depend largely on traditional technologies, mainly for metals, such as casting, forging, machining and welding. But experts believe this area is ripe for innovation and new ways of joining a wider variety of materials with greater energy and resource efficiency. Cold forming, for instance, may play a major role as a repair or advanced welding technique.

Solutions

Additives are crucial to plastic formulations. Specialty additives are one of the most dynamic segments of the plastic industry. A specialty additive insight that occurs suddenly and unexpectedly is a flash of inspiration. Knowledge or insight gained by looking into the future of polymer formulation is helpful. A sudden burst of insight about the future will produce a new and radically different way of using advanced plastic additive solutions that will open up hidden product development opportunities. Let us tour a few key polymer additive segments and explore newer trends of the future!

Olfactory solution

ScentSational Technologies, which develops/licenses olfaction packaging technologies, has introduced Compel Aroma which uses the 'Encapsulated Aroma Release' technology to add particularly engineered food-grade flavors to a plastic packaging structure to enhance a product's aroma profile. For example, Compel Aroma contained in package walls or liners can appreciably extend the period of time that a package such as coffee remains on the shelf by maintaining a desirable aroma. ScentSational has also created a technology to incorporate fragrance and flavor in single-serving beverage container closure liners designed to be consumed directly from the bottle. The technology allows the beverage bottle headspace to be filled with aromas that provide a better consumer experience. ScentSational's technology is also being used to add fragrance to the closures of shampoo, laundry detergents, and other cleaning, health and beauty products to allow consumers to sample a product's scent, without disturbing the product seal.

Packaging film advanced anti-block additives

Slip and anti-block additives are widely used to modify the surface of polymer film and sheet to facilitate performance in fabrication, packaging, and/or end-use applications. Without their use, most film would be hard to process, as the material would otherwise not slide readily over itself or other surfaces in converting, packaging and printing equipment. Film layers have a tendency to adhere when pressed together during processing or on being stacked after cutting. A range of slip and anti-block additives are available including primary, secondary, non-migratory, and other slips, in addition to organic and inorganic anti-blocks, and diverse slip and anti-block combinations. In many applications, such as single and multilayer bags, wraps and other packaging materials, these additives must have the appropriate food contact approvals. While often added directly by the resin producer, slip and anti-blocks are most commonly added by the processor via a range of master batches to adapt the additive levels to the application.

Biopolymers provide new market prospects for packaging additives such as slips and anti-blocking materials. Many of the emerging biopolymers are particularly tacky and tend to stick to themselves and to metal take-up rolls and other surfaces involved in processing. A critical factor for polylactic acid (PLA) additives is compatibility with the resin to maintain the clarity. Furthermore, some companies like Metabolix and Meredian say they will only use bio-based additives with their resins. Clariant Masterbatches has developed new CESA-slip and CESA-block masterbatches for biopolymers like PLA, employed by the packaging and film industry. The CESA-naturslip additives, based on pure naturally occurring waxes, such as beeswax, have minimal impact on the transparency and give very good slip properties with a coefficient of friction (CoF) close to that achieved using modern synthetic waxes.

Bio-based solutions and high performance bioplastic

The world's first global bio-PET (PET - polyethylene terephthalate) integrated supply chain is being established by Toyota Tsusho. The supply chain includes procurement of bio-ethanol, production of bio-mono ethylene glycol (bio-MEG), PET tolling, and bio-PET marketing. Braskem will supply the bio-ethanol from Brazil. Greenock Taiwan Corp (GTC), a 50/50 joint venture between Toyota Tsusho and China Man-Made Fiber Corporation, will produce bio-MEG using the sugar-based ethanol as feedstock. Greencol will produce the bio-MEG in a new facility in Kaohsiung, Taiwan. The bio-MEG will be handled/supplied by Toyota Tsusho to PET toll manufacturers in Asia. The off-take of bio-PET from toll manufacturers will be marketed by Toyota Tsusho to end users in Japan, Europe and the US. The companies expect to toll-produce and sell 200,000 tons/year of bio-PET.

A durable new high-performance bioplastic developed by NEC is suitable for plastic components for electronic equipment. This first-of-its kind durable new bioplastic is produced from stable non-edible plant resources. It is based on cellulose from plant stems and cardanol, a primary component of cashew nut shells. The plant stems and nut shells are abundant resources often discarded as byproducts of the agricultural processing industry. Use of these non-edible plant sources as the main components of the new bioplastic will therefore have little or no impact on the production of food crops. Cashew nuts are widely cultivated in India and Vietnam and NEC says it is assured of a stable supply of cardanol. The durable bioplastic boasts a high plant composition ratio of more than 70%. Other cellulose-based plastics are typically heavily loaded with petroleum-based plasticizers which results in a bioplastic with a low plant component ratio and poor durability including insufficient heat and water resistance or are blended with petroleum-based plastics to improve strength and thermal resistance. Cardanol has a unique molecular structure that consists of a rigid phenol component and a flexible, hydrophobic, linear hydrocarbon component. Cellulose is the main ingredient of the bioplastic and is bonded with the oil-like cardanol which has been modified to enhance its reactivity. NEC expects the new bioplastic to be commercialized shortly at a price lower than PLA and competitive to petroleum-based plastics. NEC believes that the durability achieved by the new bioplastic will make it highly suitable for electronics applications.

A page is being taken from the computer industry to spur innovation and drive biopolymers more widely into injection moulding applications. Nature Works is making formulation and compounding procedures for its high-heat resistant high-impact bio-resin, Ingeo 3801X, which is openly available. The company has 'drawn back the curtain' on the development of the grade to share the technology and provide transparency on how the solution was arrived at, including what was used to tailor properties/processing characteristics and why was it done. Information is also openly available about high-heat formulation, Ingeo HHIM 670-82-01. With formulation in hand, independent specialty resin companies and brand owners with captive operations will be in a position to use Ingeo as the foundation for bio-based injection moulded products and components. Nature Works also expects the details of the formulation can serve as a basis for R&D in further tailoring bio-based solutions for the semi-durable plastics market. The company has also taken a similar 'pull back the curtain' approach with its foam grade material, 8051D, but as that grade had just a small group of potential users, it was done more on a one-to-one basis. Nature Works is now offering for sale a range of polymer-grade lactides. Lactide partners can also take advantage of a new Ingeo licensee package. Under select terms, the company will supply access to trademarks and application patents needed to support and enable the wider adoption of Ingeo biopolymers.

Highly heat resistant PLA moulding compound, MBA900H, co-developed by Panasonic Electric Works and Teijin Ltd., is composed of 80% plant-based renewable feedstock. The compound has significantly reduced moulding cycle time around half of that of conventional PLA compounds. Conventional PLA has low heat resistance and limited injection-moulding capability because of its longer moulding cycle time. Other moulding compounds have been developed by mixing PLA with petroleum-based plastics, but attaining the desired levels of heat resistance and mouldability has required a high ratio of oil-based plastic. In Teijin's 'Biofront' bioplastic, a highly heat-resistant PLA is used in the compound. Teijin's Biofront stereo-complex PLA has a melting point of approximately 210°C, which is significantly higher than that of the conventional PLA. It also shows better hydrolytic stability and achieves semi-crystallization in just 20-25% of the time required with that of the conventional PLA. The stereo-complex PLA, made with conventional 'left handed' poly-L-lactic acid combined with its 'right-handed' poly-D-lactic acid that has a much higher heat resistance. 8Biofront PLA of 50/50 L and D lactides achieves a semi-crystalline resin state with a melting point 40°C higher than that of the conventional PLA, and is on par with the heat resistance of petroleum-based PBT. Panasonic Electric Works' proprietary compound-design and production technologies were also used in the development. The compound will initially be used in the housing of cell phones and other mobile devices and digital consumer electronics. Panasonics' initial goal is 1,000 tons of annual production. Teijin operates a Biofront demonstration plant with a capacity of 1,000 tons/year and expects to increase its capacity to 5,000 tons/year.

Formulations and transparency

Solasorb, a novel type of inorganic ultra violet (UV) light absorber from Croda Polymer Additives is based on ultra fine metal oxides (TiO_2 and ZnO) that provide stable dispersion, low migration, and long-term protection. In comparison with traditional nano-particle additives, this UV protection material is said to deliver:

- Low migration
- Long-term UV protection
- Greater dispersion
- Minimal effect on transparency

Careful particle size control yields a good UV absorbance coupled with significantly improved transparency compared to other metal oxide powders. Its use in plastics for packaging applications reduces the color change in cosmetics and personal care products, and prevents vitamin loss and development of off-tastes and odors in beverages.

NanoArc Antimony Tin Oxide (ATO) nano-particle additives by Nanophase Technologies Corporation can be incorporated into clear film and sheet to absorb infra-red (IR) but not visible light. It provides this benefit by absorbing energy in the near-IR region and reflecting energy at longer IR wavelengths, while maintaining excellent transparency in the visible region. In products like skylights, it prevents heating of the interior space. The incorporation of NanoArc ATO into surface coatings is an effective means of managing radiant heat without adversely impacting the optical clarity or other desirable physical properties of the article on which it is applied.

Green plastic

While green plastic offers principles for the development of 'greener' reagents and alternatives and more benign routes to synthetic methodologies, it does not have the capacity to bring about a radical change. An agreement has to be arrived at between the policy makers and the chemical practitioners in order to give green plastic the power it rightly deserves. And a policy needs to be framed to guide the practitioners, so that satisfactory efficiency as well as environmental cleanliness is achieved. It is reiterated that the espousal the cause for and adoption of green plastic must involve not only the academia or academic intelligentsia, but also the science and technology agencies and administrators. It is only through a synchronized movement of these apparently segregated entities that we can bring about a reform movement in plastic and chemical technology. The role of the academia is to bring about a mass understanding about the pertinence of green plastic. This body must also take upon itself to device appropriate educational material for different levels of curricular instruction. The R&D and the science and technology agencies that are responsible for the funding of scientific activities in the country must encourage and give preference to the development of greener science and technology. In order to ensure global environmental protection, while keeping scientific and economic development on the forefront, the policy makers should understand the role of 'green' science and technology and make pollution prevention, rather than pollution control, their slogan. Though it is true that many industries and research organizations are yet to implement the principles of green plastic, nevertheless some of them have begun to realize that the 'think green' culture is more than just a fashion. In fact, the winds of changes have already started blowing and the more successful plastic researchers and chemical technologists will like to appreciate and apply the values of green plastic in innovation, application and education.

The objective of this book, as evident from the title, is to suggest changes to some existing procedures. The suggestions made in this book are on the basis of the outcomes of a study. This study was conducted with primary data. Innovation, SPCs, the right use of scientific methods and improvements in organizational culture are the main variables taken into consideration for optimization, in terms of costing and production. In this study, the impact of all the above processes are studied independently and, finally, a case study of these suggestions are implemented together is presented. The process for the study was implemented in the existing systems, and the differences were noted. As for tangible comparison is concerned, it will be easy to demonstrate it in terms of time and money. Thus,, these two parameters were used most to study the results. This is because, any study will turn out to be limitless if we try to research and present each and every aspect of the manufacturing process; thus it is imperative we select a few. The processes used for the study, like 'Plastic Injection Molding' are only the beginning of a future, and only sky is the limit to improve upon this work from the perspectives of Physicists, Process Makers, Innovators, and Entrepreneurs.

2

APPROACHES TO PRODUCTION: AN ASSESSMENT

PRODUCTION AND MANUFACURING PROCESS

The current trend in production is that it is moving towards adaptable manufacturing processes for extensive manufacturing, numerous determinations and machining operations on the same work piece. Additionally, the production processes have to produce items that must meet the obliged quality. There is need of high precision and accuracy machine apparatus that can deliver multi-mixture, multi-particular items in a short span of lead time and also with higher process capacities. Along these lines, today's process control method needs to empower the plant with hardware and supplies to create multi-assortment, multi-particular items in lesser time with higher process capacities. High process ability is imperative to the production of such a large number of little-size complex-outline extra parts. Although Statistical Process Control (SPC) is being used nowadays in numerous businesses, yet execution of SPC is becoming even an extreme assignment for the shop-floor workers. The inspiration that has come along the way is that eventually whatever sort of process-control instrument is actually used, it must oblige a foreordained set of activity arrangements for controlling the manufacturing processes up to the level which results in a 'higher process ability'.

A manufacturing process is concerned with the change of a set of information that converts crude materials into the coveted yields. The yields are, for the most part, expected to meet some obliged measurable targets. Accurate conformance is impractical because of elements which cause the process yield variables to stray from the target. These elements may be varieties in the inputs or varieties in the process itself. Varieties in the inputs, for the most part, happen because of some assignable or extraordinary reasons. Varieties in the process itself happen because of a few unsettling influences known as 'chance' or 'normal' reasons.

OPTIMIZATION FOR MANUFACTURING PROCESS

In enhancing the money matters of machining operations, the part of cutting conditions – for example, food rate, cutting velocity and profundity of cut have long been studied. F.W. Taylor (1907) demonstrated that an ideal or financial cutting velocity exists, which expands the material evacuation rate.

Gilbert (1950) considered the enhancement of machining parameters, in turn, taking the most extreme production rate and the least production cost as the criteria.

Brewer and Rueda (1963) completed streamlined ideal dissection for non-ferrous materials. For cast iron (CI) and steels, they utilized the measure of least machining expense.

A section of the generally utilized methods within enhancement are Ordinary Hereditary Calculation, Molecule Swarm Improvement and Reproduced Toughening.

Armarego and Brown (1969) explored unconstrained machine-parameter enhancement, utilizing differential mathematics.

(Niebel and Freivalds, 2003) talked about the stream outline that gives the most important data of a manufacturing process. It is a realistic portrayal of the development of materials, starting with one movement, and then onto the next.

The stream example of the materials and apparatuses could be drawn on a current design arrangement of the plant region. Divisions or territories of significance could be referenced by numbers on the outline. Stream graphs deal with the disposal and decrease of any concealed expenses that are connected with a particular action of the process. Activity blockage regions and backtracking of materials can be made obvious on the stream outline, which can help in the improvement of an ideal plant-design selection. Bottlenecks can additionally be distinguished on a stream graph. A bottleneck is an asset that confines the limit of the process and can, along these lines, be seen as the pacesetter of the stream rate in the manufacturing framework. Enhanced bottlenecks will prompt an enhanced framework.

As indicated by Niebel *et al.* (2003), the measure of tooling that is most worthwhile relies upon:

- The Production Amount
- Repeat Business
- Labour
- Delivery Prerequisites
- Required Capital

Lack of planning and wasteful tooling prompts expanded setup times and costs. A tooling assessment agenda could be utilized to evaluate the sum and state of the currently-used instruments and the devices which are required.

Institutionalized supplies and tooling ought to be at a level that is consistent with the desired outcomes. Device examination decides the viability of specific devices and their particular functionalities. It is imperative to verify that the right tooling is utilized for the right occupation, so that the nature of the item is not influenced adversely.

As indicated by Niebel *et al.* (2003), "...the goal of the manufacturing administrator is to deliver a quality item, on timetable, at the most reduced conceivable expense, with least capital venture and a greatest of worker fulfillment." An investigation of conceivable strategies has been carried out to find out which routines would create this finished result. Niebel *et al.* (2003) expresses, "...basically all operations could be enhanced if sufficient study is given to them."

The six essential inquiries made to accumulate realities are: what, why, how, who, where and when. Nine efficient methodologies have been designed to help with the investigation of the truths accumulated. These nine methodologies are:

- Operation Reason
- Part Plan
- Tolerances and Particulars
- Material
- Manufacture Grouping and Process
- Setup and Apparatuses
- Taking Care of Material
- Plant Format
- Work Plan

The configuration destination, which comes before most building outline exercises, is just to minimize the expense of production or to augment the production effectiveness. An improvement calculation is a methodology which is executed iteratively by contrasting different results till the ideal or acceptable result is reached. Without waiting for the the best result, and by looking at a few outline results is a backhanded method for accomplishing enhancement in numerous mechanical configuration exercises. There is no possibility to ensure an ideal result with this kind of a shortsighted methodology. Improvement calculations, in reality, start with one or more outline results supplied by the client, and after that, new plan results and relative hunt spaces are iteratively checked keeping in mind the end goal to accomplish the genuine, ideal result.

Jong and Hartog (2007) expresses, "Administrative abilities restricted for associations to wind up more inventive is to gain by their representatives' capacity to advance". The administration of workforce obliges an above-normal state of individuals' administrative abilities. It is vital to have workers who are prepared and propelled, as it will specifically affect the nature of the item and the gainfulness of the association.

A study (Jong and Hartog, 2007) demonstrates that there are 13 practices that a pioneer can embrace to push advancement in the work environment:

- Innovative part displaying
- Intellectual incitement
- Stimulating learning dispersion
- Providing vision
- Consulting
- Delegating
- Support for advancement
- Organizing criticism
- Recognition
- Rewards
- Providing assets
- Monitoring
- Tasks

As indicated by Jacobs *et al.* (2009), "...great housekeeping involves keeping just essential things in the work territory, that there is a spot for everything and that everything is clean and in a steady state of preparation. At the point when great housekeeping is set up, neatness, quality control, security and pride will come about at the end of the day."

The 5s philosophy is focused around the following five Japanese acronyms:

- *Seiri* – Association
- *Seiton* – Tidiness
- *Seiso* – Cleaning
- *Seiketsu* – Institutionalization
- *Shitsuke* – Discipline

The point of 5s is to imbibe these qualities into the work environment. The essential goal of 5s is to make a sheltered and solid work environment where benefits could be expanded – the key necessities of profit, quality, costs, conveyance, security, and assurance.

Jacobs *et al.* (2009) has characterized assembly-line adjusting as the issue of appointing all the undertakings to an arrangement of workstations so that every workstation is as close to each other as possible in the workstation process duration, such that sitting time over all workstations are minimized.

OPTIMIZATION STRATEGIES

The most recent systems for enhancement of production incorporate fuzzy logic, scatter search technique, genetic algorithm, Taguchi technique and response surface methodology.

Fuzzy Logic

Fuzzy logic has an extraordinary capacity to catch human matter of factual thinking, choice making and different aspects of human perception. Kosko (1997) has demonstrated that it beats all the constraints.

Dubiousness in the coefficients and stipulations may be characteristically displayed by fuzzy logic. Demonstration by fuzzy logic opens up another approach to enhance cutting-edge conditions and prudent apparatus determination further.

Methodology

According to Klir and Yuan (1998), fuzzy logic includes a fuzzy impedance motor and a fuzzification-defuzzification module. The fuzzification module communicates the information variables as fuzzy enrollment qualities focused around different participation capacities and manages in phonetic structures. For example, if cutting energy is high and machining time is high, then the device wear is high, are formed on the premise of test perceptions. Taking into account every rule, an inference could be drawn on yield evaluation and participation esteem. Deductions got from different principles are consolidated to touch base at a definite choice. The participation values, therefore, got are defuzzified utilizing different techniques to acquire genuine quality, say of flank wear.

Genetic Algorithm (GA)

These are the algorithms focused around mechanics of characteristic choice and common genetics, which are more hearty and more inclined to hog the ideal spot worldwide. It is a result of this gimmick that GA experiences result space beginning from a gathering of focuses and not from a solitary point. The cutting conditions are encoded as qualities by double encoding to apply GA in streamlining of machining parameters. A set of qualities are joined together to structure chromosomes, and used to perform the essential systems in GA, for example, hybrid and transformation.

Hybrid is the operation to trade some pieces of two-chromosomes to produce a new posterity, which is vital while investigating the entire search space quickly. Change is connected after hybrid to give a little arbitrariness to the new chromosomes. To assess every individual or chromosome, the encoded cutting conditions are decoded from the chromosomes and are utilized to foresee machining execution measures. Wellness or goal capacity is a capacity required in the improvement procedure and determination of cutting edge in the genetic algorithm. Ideal after-effects of cutting conditions are acquired by correlation of estimations of goal capacities among all people after various emphases. Other than weighting variables and stipulations, suitable parameters of GA are obliged to work effectively. The GA streamlining system is focused around machining execution forecast models created from an exhaustive arrangement of hypothetical dissection, exploratory database and numerical techniques. The GA parameters alongside significant destination capacities and set of machining execution stipulations are forced on GA streamlining system to give ideal cutting conditions.

Implementation of GA

Above all, the variables are encoded as n-bit parallel numbers relegated consecutively as chromosome strings. To execute imperatives in GA, punishments are given to people out of imperative. On the off-chance that an individual is out of imperative, its wellness will be appointed as zero. Since people are chosen to mate as per wellness worth, zero wellness people would not get to be folks. In this way, most people in the cutting edge are guaranteed in achievable locales limited via stipulations.

The GA is instated by arbitrarily selecting people in the full scope of variables. Individuals are chosen to be folks of the cutting edge as per their wellness value. The bigger the wellness esteem, the more noteworthy is their plausibility of being chosen as parents. Wang and Jawahir (2004) have utilized this technique for advancement of processing machine parameters.

Kuo and Yen (2002) have utilized a GA-based parameter-tuning algorithm for multidimensional movement control of a machine numerical control machine device.

Scatter Search Technique (SS)

This technique starts from systems for joining together choice tenets and surrogate constraints. SS is totally summed up and is issue-free since it has no prohibitive suspicions about destination capacity, parameter set and stipulation set. It could be effectively adjusted to upgrade machining operations under different monetary criteria and various viable imperatives. It can get results close to ideal, inside sensible execution time on the PC.

Possibly, it might be stretched out as an on-line quality control methodology for advancing machining parameters focused around signs originating from sensors.

Methodology

Most importantly, machining models are obliged to focus on the ideal machining parameters including cutting velocity, food rate and profundity of cut, with a specific end goal to minimize the unit creation cost. Unit generation expense could be isolated into four fundamental expense components:

- Cutting the cost by a genuine cut in the time
- Machine unmoving cost, because of stacking and emptying operation and sitting device movement cost
- Device substitution cost
- Instrument cost

For the enhancement of unit generation cost, reasonable obligations which display the state of machining methods need to be considered. The requirements that are forced amid machining operations are:

- Parameter imperative – Scopes of cutting velocity, food rate and profundity of cut
- Instrument life demand – Passable estimations of flank wear width and hole wear profundity
- Working obligation – Most extreme passable cutting energy, power accessible on machine apparatus and surface completion prerequisite

An enhancement model for multi-pass turning operation might be defined. The multi-pass turning model is a compelling nonlinear programming issue with numerous variables (machining variables). The introductory answer for SS is picked in a random way. The pointed out parameters by the client must be given. The experimentation might be run on a PC with a Pentium 800 MHz processor. The computational results accept the point of interest of SS as far as result quality and computational necessity is concerned.

Taguchi Technique

Genichi Taguchi is a Japanese engineer who has been dynamic in the change of Japan's modern items and courses of action since the late 1940s. He has created both the rationality and philosophy for procedure or item quality change that depends intensely on measurable ideas and instruments, particularly measurable composed examinations. Numerous Japanese firms have attained incredible accomplishment by applying his methods. Wu (1982) has reported that a large number of specialists have performed countless trials focused around his teachings. Sullivan (1987), reports that Taguchi has got some of the Japan's most prestigious grants for quality accomplishments, including the Deming Prize. In 1986, Taguchi got the most prestigious prize from the Global Innovation Organization – The Willard F. Rockwell Decoration for Incredibleness in Engineering. Taguchi's significant commitment has included joining together designing and measurable techniques to attain fast upgrades in expense and quality by upgrading item plan and assembling procedures.

Kackar and Shoemaker (1986) watched that parameter outline decreases execution variety by decreasing the impact of the wellsprings of variety as opposed to by controlling them. It is consequently an extremely savvy technique for enhancing building configuration. Byrne and Taguchi (1987) brought up that the key component for accomplishing with panache and ease is parameter outline. Through parameter outline, levels of item and methodology variables are resolved, such that the item's useful qualities are advanced and the impact of clamor components is minimized. Taguchi (1989) depicted that quality designing incorporates all phases of item/process improvement: framework plan, parameter outline and tolerance outline.

Sullivan (1987) reported that the expression 'Taguchi techniques' (TM) allude to the parameter outline, tolerance plan, quality misfortune capacity, on-line quality control, configuration of investigations utilizing orthogonal show, and the technique connected to assess measuring frameworks.

Pignatiello (1988) recognizes two different parts of the TM – the methodology of Taguchi and the strategies of Taguchi. Taguchi strategies allude to the accumulation of particular techniques and those techniques that are utilized by Genichi Taguchi. The Taguchi methodology refers to the applied system or structure for arranging an item or procedure configuration test.

Ryan (1988) and Benton (1991) reported that Taguchi locations plan designing (disconnected from the net) and assembling (online) quality. This, in a broad sense, separates TM from factual methodology control (SPC), which is essentially an online quality control system.

Barker (1990) reported that since 1983, after Taguchi's relationship developed with the top organizations and foundations in USA (AT&T, Ringer Laoratories, Xerox, Lawrence Establishment of Engineering (LIT), Passage Engine Organization and so on), his routines have been known as a radical methodology for quality, experimental plan and building.

Taguchi's thoughts could be refined into two principal ideas:

- Quality misfortunes must be characterized as deviations from targets, not conformance to self-assertive details (Benton, 1991).
- Attaining high-framework quality levels financially obliges quality to be outlined into the item. Quality is outlined, not produced, into the item (Daetz, 1987 and Taguchi, 1989).

Lin *et al.* (1990) expressed that Taguchi techniques speak about another rationality. Quality is measured by the deviation of a useful trademark from its target esteem. Clamors (uncontrolled variables) can result in such deviations bringing about loss of value. Taguchi routines help to evacuate the impact of commotions.

SCHEDULING PROBLEM OPTIMIZATION

Hanssmann and Whess (1960) utilized Direct Programming (DP). Direct Programming is a numerical technique for deciding an approach to accomplish the best conclusion, like greatest benefit or most minimal cost in a given model. Direct Programming is a particular instance of numerical advancement.

Held and Karp (1962) have proposed Element Programming as an understood enumerative search system. This could be seen as a sort of separation and vanquishing technique, with a specific end goal to tackle a huge issue, disaggregate it into a few little autonomous sub issues, and take care of all the little sub issues and keep them for later utilization.

Ignall and Schrage (1965) created limb and headed algorithms for the change stream shop issue with make compass minimization.

Bomberger (1966) displayed the DP methodology to parcel planning issues. He considered the creation and planning of diverse 'things' over the same office on a monotonous premise. The office in the framework is such that the 'stand out thing' could be created and the methodology applied at a time. The 'thing' delivered is connected with the setup expense and setup time. The interest rate for each 'thing' is known and it will be consistent over an endless arranging horizon. All requests must be met.

Campbell *et al.* (1970) connected heuristic algorithm in stages. Lockett and Muhlemann (1972) utilized the limb and headed algorithm for booking employments with grouping ward setup times on a solitary processor to minimize the aggregate number of hardware progressions. The algorithm was prohibitive computationally.

Crowin and Esogbue (1974) considered the two distinctive stream-shop planning issues. These emerge when, in a two-machine issue, one machine is described by grouping ward setup times. The destination is to focus a calendar that minimizes making compass. In the wake of securing the ideal of stage timetables for both of these issues, a proficient DP detailing is produced for each of them.

GA-based algorithms are propelled by Darwin's hypothesis of *Characteristic choice and survival of the fittest*. These were imagined by Holland (1975).

Rinnooy Kan (1976) showed that a regular approach to assault booking issues is by planning them as scientific programming models. The results found were not agreeable. The lion's share of these techniques is not able to attain possible answers for some issues. Accordingly, these routines are of restricted functional utilization.

Panwalkar *et al.* (1977) have given a point by point clarification of some of these dispatching tenets.

Tripathy (1980), Arani *et al.* (1988), and Sadykov and A. Wolsey (2006) have connected IP on vehicle planning issue. The results were better.

Gupta (1982) utilized a scientific model focused around the limb and bound technique to tackle static planning issues including n occupations and m machines for minimizing the expense of machine setting. He expected that the set up times were arrangement subordinate. It is excluded in handling times. The algorithm was just used to tackle little size issues. It gave knowledge into the structure of ideal results. These could be utilized to devise great heuristic principles. Heuristic principles are, for the most part, more fitting to tackle expansive size booking issues where computational deliberations build quickly with issue size for streamlining techniques.

Kirkpatrick *et al.* (1983) connected SA to combinatorial streamlining issues.

Hundal *et al.* (1988) utilized heuristic algorithm for the stream-shop booking issue.

Mccormick *et al.* (1989) utilized a Profile Fitting (PF) heuristic algorithm. It is focused around the flight times of the occupations figured after each employment has been planned.

Goldberg (1989) utilized GAs for planning issues. In the GA-based methodology, the different stages like assessment, selection, crossover and change are more than once executed after introduction until a halting paradigm is met. The algorithm chips away at different results all the while.

Taillard (1990) demonstrated that irregular pair astute swapping is computationally more costly contrasted with the arbitrary insertion system. He indicated tentatively that irregular pair insightful swapping improves the ideal result than the arbitrary insertion strategy.

Rajendran and Chaudhuri (1992) utilized a heuristic algorithm to minimize stream time for a stream-shop booking issue. It utilizes three heuristic criteria: (i) It manages the whole of unmoving times; (ii) It fuses the aggregate of unmoving times and the holding up times; and (iii) It incorporates the finishing times of the incomplete timetable at different stages.

Berry *et al.* (1993) utilized valuable techniques called information-based or AI-based frameworks.

Taillard (1993) utilized ground dwelling insect State Advancement Algorithms (ACOA) to assess upper headed qualities for make compass consider and suitable just for the little estimated issues.

Zegordi *et al.* (1995) demonstrated that a decent set of parameters can bring about much snappier meeting to the ideal result.

Marett and Wright (1996) looked at the execution of TS algorithm and SA algorithm for multi-target stream-shop planning issues. They found that result obtained by utilizing SA algorithm were superior to TS algorithm.

Skillet and Fan (1997) utilized limb and headed algorithm for the same issue. They utilized strength properties to decrease the measure of the issue. The algorithm could tackle all the issues up to 18 employments.

Chen *et al.* (1998) connected DP methodology to the unwinding issue of booking. It concerns the utilization of Lagrangean unwinding for complex booking issues. Ideal result has been found for single and parallel machine issue by utilizing this technique. It comprises unwinding limit obligations utilizing Lagrange multipliers. The loose issue might be disintegrated into autonomous occupation level sub issues.

Voss *et al.* (1999) utilized a meta-heuristic algorithm as an iterative expert method that aids and changes the operations of subordinate heuristics to effectively deliver great results.

De Castro and Timmis (2003) utilized Counterfeit Resistant Framework (AIS) Algorithm. AIS is a versatile heuristic technique roused by the human-safe framework. The two basic angles in the invulnerable reaction instrument are: (i) colonel determination guideline and (ii) partiality development.

Engin and Doyen (2004) utilized an AIS-based heuristic for half-bred stream shops. They connected their algorithm to the benchmark issues for mixture stream shops. This algorithm performs better than Extension and Bound algorithms.

Rajendran and Ziegler (2005) utilized two Acoas to minimize the aggregate stream time in change stream shops. The algorithms create a starting seed arrangement. It likewise does a nearby search at the end of every cycle.

Noorul Haq and Radha Ramanan (2006) utilized ANN to minimize bi criteria of make compass and aggregate stream time in stream shop nature. They demonstrated that ANN accomplishes an answer quality better than that of conventional heuristics or in any event practically identical to it. They reasoned that ANN incrementally enhances the result quality with the build in quantities of preparing models.

Chakraborty and Laha (2007) utilized the NEH algorithm for make compass minimization issue in change stream shop planning. Their computational study uncovered the huge change in the nature of the result while keeping up the same algorithmic many-sided quality.

STATSTICAL PROCESS CONTROL

SPC instruments might be executed to diminish the varieties in the yield that can corrupt yield nature of products. SPC is a strategy for quality control which utilizes statistical routines. SPC is connected to screening and control of a process.

Observing and controlling the process guarantees that it works at its maximum capacity. At its maximum capacity, the process can make however much acclimating product as could reasonably be expected with a base (if not a disposal) of waste (adjust or refuse). SPC might be connected to any process where the "adjusting product" (product meeting particulars) yield could be measured.

Key instruments utilized as a part of SPC incorporate control graphs; a concentrate on consistent change; and the configuration of trials. A case of a process where SPC is connected is assembling lines. The application of SPC to a process intends to bring about the end of process waste. This, thusly, wipes out the requirement for the process venture of post-assembling review.

The accomplishment of SPC depends not just on the ability with which it is connected, additionally on how suitable or manageable the process is to SPC. Now and again, it might be hard to judge when the application of SPC is proper.

Statistical Process Control (SPC) helps us observing a process persistently. The motivation behind control outlining is to demonstrate when the process is working as expected and when is definitely not. Some proper remedial measures need to be taken at whatever point fundamental.

For the sort diagram presented by Shewhart (1931, 1939), a wild indicator is given by the graph when the detail computed from a specimen falls outside control limits. These cutoff points are normally situated at ± 3 standard mistakes of the plotted fact from a centerline at its chronicled normal worth. The recipe for the figuring of the standard lapse is typically focused around a distributional presumption, e.g., the binomial model for a p-outline used to screen extents. The ensuing control cutoff points are alluded to as "three-sigma" limits. The figuring of any statistical measure of execution requires a supposition about the type of the likelihood conveyance of the quality trademark.

Shewhart, W. A. (1939) said that the application of SPC includes three fundamental sets of exercises:

- Understanding of the process. This is attained by business process mapping.
- Measuring the wellsprings of variety aided by the utilization of control diagrams and
- Dispensing with assignable (exceptional) wellsprings of variety

Burr (1967) demonstrated that non typicality seems to have little impact on the estimations of control outline constants. To first utilize a control diagram as a part of practice, on the other hand, no suspicions of ordinariness or freedom about whether need to be made. Truth be told, distributional suppositions can't even be checked before a control graph is at first connected in a Stage 1 circumstance on the grounds that one might not have process soundness. As one works inside Stage 1 to uproot assignable reasons and to accomplish process steadiness, the manifestation of the conjectured underlying likelihood conveyance gets to be more imperative in deciding proper control limits and in evaluating process ability. To decipher a graph in Stage 1, experts need to be mindful that the likelihood of indicators can differ impressively relying upon the state of the underlying dissemination for a stable process, the level of autocorrelation in the information, and the quantity of examples.

Taguchi (1981) pushed lessening of variability until it gets to be monetarily disadvantageous to lessen it further. To utilize a control diagram, for example, the X-outline to screen the process mean or the R-graph to screen variability, specimens are assumed control time and estimations of a detail are plotted.

Deming (1986) and numerous others have contended that gathering particular points of confinement is not sufficient to guarantee great quality and that the variability of the quality attributes ought to be diminished such that, as Deming (1986) depicts it, "Details are lost into the great beyond." Subsequently, for some quality qualities, quality change relates to focusing the likelihood dispersion of the quality trademark at a target esteem and diminishing variability.

D.J. Wheeler and D.S. Chambers (1992) expressed that variety exists in all processes. On the off-chance that a regular reason is the main kind of variety that exists in the process, the process is said to be 'in control' and stable. It is additionally unsurprising that inside the situated breaking points, i.e., the likelihood of any future result falling inside the cutoff points could be expressed roughly. On the other hand, if an extraordinary reason variety exists inside the process then the process is portrayed as being crazy and precarious. It implies that variety exists all over the place, processes showing just regular reason variety are unsurprising inside statistical cutoff points, and uncommon reason variety ought to be wiped out if conceivable.

Henry R. Neave (1992) specified that the control diagram might be seen as a feature of a destination and a trained approach that empowers right choices with regard to control of the process, including whether to change process control parameters. The process parameters ought to never be balanced for a process that is in control, as this will bring about debased process execution results.

J. Oakland (2002) said that in mass producing, customarily, the nature of a completed article is guaranteed by post-fabricating review of the product. Each article (or an example of articles from a production part) may be acknowledged or rejected according to how well it reaches its plan details. Conversely, SPC utilizes statistical instruments to watch the execution of the production process to foresee huge varieties which may bring about the production of a sub-standard article. A wellspring of variety at any one purpose of a production process can be categorized as one of two classes given below.

- 'Normal' - in some cases alluded to as 'typical' or 'chance' wellsprings of variety
- 'Assignable' - at times alluded to as 'unique' wellsprings of variety

A process capacity examination may be performed on a stable process to foresee the capability of the process to create an 'accommodating product' later on. Roberta Russell and Bernard W. Taylor (2006) said that a process that is steady and however working outside of sought restraints needs to be enhanced through a purposeful exertion to comprehend the reason for current execution and, in a general sense, enhances the process. SPC is normally actualized to administrations where the nature of imperfection is diverse, and the administration deformity is a disappointment to meet client prerequisites, screen time and client fulfillment.

Farzana Sultana, Nahid Islam Razive and Abdullahil Azeem (June 2009) specified that in a nature's domain, the SPC apparatus is utilized for constant change of the production volume and also quality which prompts accomplishing fabricating fabulousness.

Rami Hikmat Fouad and Adnan Mukattash (2010) said that variable control graphs are utilized to study a process when the attribute is an estimation, for instance, process duration, processing time, holding up time, most astounding, region, temperature, expense or income. Estimation information gives more data than quality information: therefore, variables outlines are more touchy in distinguishing uncommon reason variety than are characteristic graphs. A standout amongst the most regularly utilized pair of outlines is the X bar-diagram and the R-outline. Through the utilization of control diagrams, comparable increases might be acknowledged in the assembling segment. Clients of control outlines report reserve funds in scrap, including material and work, lower revamp expenses, lessened investigations, higher product quality, more steady part qualities, more noteworthy administrator certainty, and lower troubleshooting,

QUALITY CONSIDERATIONS IN MANUFACTURING

As of late, essential changes in the industry's aggressive edge has been putting solid weights on consistent change needs, quickening the leap forward in quality administration issues. Subsequently, over a year ago, numerous associations (little, medium measured, vast, from industry, and from administration) have grasped aggregate quality administration (TQM) as the administration theory that runs their key arrangement. In the meantime, concentrated writing on TQM has been developing in the most recent decades. Through an exhaustive investigation of writing, distributed basically by the quality masters and other quality issues specialists, the pioneer study did by Saraph *et al.* (1989) performed a past extraction of one hundred and twenty hierarchical solutions for a successful TQM execution and in this way bunched them into eight classes of basic achievement elements (CSF), characterizing these, as discriminating issues in managerial arranging/activity that must be polished to accomplish a viable quality administration.

In assembling businesses, the general term 'quality' alludes to what quality administration writing partitions into the two corresponding classifications of nature of configuration and nature of conformance. While the nature of outline concentrates on how the product configuration meets buyers' necessities, the nature of conformance is concerned with whether the quality created and given to the shopper meets the planned outline. Both the quality levers act together to focus the quality seen by the purchaser. Yet, while the nature of configuration is a basic piece of product quality, it just has a minor effect on the tradeoffs between assembling processes and review methods. The subject of this theory is thus the best held steady. Then again, the nature of conformance assumes a focal part in assembling process and examination method of determination.

All assembling processes are blemished and have a related non-conformance rate. Makers looking to accomplish higher nature of conformance have an extensive variety of choices to browse. These might be partitioned into two classes – enhancing delivered nature of conformance by means of imperfection anticipation and enhancing nature of conformance conveyed to the client through assessment.

Conceivable systems for avoidance incorporate assembling process change or change, specialist preparing and supplier review programs. The 1980s saw a surge of enthusiasm toward creating and actualizing projects adapted at enhancing the assembling process nature of conformance. The most eminent philosophies proposed from that point forward incorporate Aggregate Quality Administration (TQM), Toyota Production Frameworks' Kaizen and Six Sigma from Motorola.

For a settled decision of assembling process, the key lever controlling the ensuing cordial nature of conformance is assessment. The objective of the review is to distinguish delivered desserts before they are conveyed to the client. Indeed, inside examination itself, an extensive variety of methodology options are accessible.

As focused by Dale (1994), organizations grasping TQM standards must verify that each associate has an acceptable vision about what the association anticipates from him and about the way his errands fit into the general exercises.

As per Quip and Button (1999), TQM added another measurement to quality administration issues: the redefinition of value from the client's perspective, in light of commercial center confirmations. As pushed by the creators, through such emotional movement in point of view, quality may be seen as a compelling focused weapon and included in firms' 'key' arranging.

Actually, as highlighted by Brah *et al.* (2002), TQM cannot be seen as a snappy settle way, focusing on that its prosperity includes a long haul ideal model transformation through critical hierarchical progressions

A few perceptions recommend clear concerns from a large portion of the SME segment about quality matters, as a rule, and about the vitality of each collaborator's inclusion in projects situated to quality change, specifically.

Amongst others, these procedures may contrast in the decision of review game plan inside an arrangement of assembling processes, screening breaking points, assessment techniques and additionally examination designation (from 0% to 100%).

COST MANAGEMENT VIEWPOINT

Mass customization has been characterized as the capability to outline and alter production products at a large-scale manufacturing productivity and pace. Customization and mass customization are regularly supported in light of the fact that distinctive clients can give diverse qualities to the same product. Clients adopt these diverse peculiarities and execution, and one size does not fit all holds true any longer.

There are various illustrations of diverse mass redone products, in which Dell stands out as an example. In any case, a large number of studies focuses on buyer merchandize, and these have regularly demonstrated them either as a showcasing or an operations view, despite the fact that there are a few studies that have concentrated on administration bookkeeping. The results are opposing. A few scholars propose advanced administration bookkeeping frameworks, in the same way as action-based costing, and others cannot discover them to be legitimate.

Juran (1951), in his literature, discussed the most common methodology for accommodating the contending goals of expense minimization and nature of conformance augmentation at the expense of value (COQ) approach. An extensive variety of research papers in the fields of modern or quality building examine the hypothesis behind COQ.

In the interim, the operations research order addresses particular measurements inside assessment procedure streamlining for a settled decision of manufacturing process. Most papers in this field consider both expense and quality parts of assessment, though to different degrees. The accompanying segment will outline research-to-date relating to both the hypothesis of COQ and investigation procedure advancement. This segment closes with an examination of how the writing addresses or does not address expense and nature of conformance tradeoffs and additionally the measurements utilized for manufacturing process and review system choice.

The COQ methodology offers an approach to accommodate producers to clashing goals of augmenting nature of conformance and minimizing expense. By connecting expenses to nature of conformance, this methodology changes the double target into one goal of expense of value minimization. This takes into account a less demanding examination of manufacturing process and investigation method choices.

Yet there is no single meaning of COQ and its constituent expense components. The main formal meaning of expense of value could be followed back to *Quality Control Handbook* which incorporates the fact that all the expenses would vanish if no imperfections were delivered. From that point forward, the idea of COQ has experienced an arrangement of adjustments and refinements. Expense and quality tradeoffs might be seen by analyzing the relationship between the diverse expense classifications inside COQ. At a more elevated amount, one can recognize COQ writing that participates in a hypothetical discourse of the assumed connections and writing that is more connected, either exact or logical in nature.

In the event that we take the meaning of administration as a movement as a given, then there is a clear costing strategy for administration, named action-based costing (ABC). In ABC, the product expenses could be dictated by allotting the expenses of exercises to a product that utilizes those exercises. The ABC system sees movement as a task that is embraced to make or convey a product or an administration. Action-based costing is particularly valuable when costs in roundabout and help assets are high, and a difference exists in products, clients, and processes (Kaplan & Cooper 1998). In an instance of mass customization, there are surely differences in products and clients. True, processes vary, despite the fact that there is a plan to institutionalize these. In an instance of mass altered administration, products are characterized as processes so that the assorted qualities originate from that point.

QUALITY FUNCTION DEPLOYMENT (QFD) IN MANUFACTURING

QFD was started in the late 1960s to 1970s, in Japan, by the Teacher Yoji (Akao, 1972). It is a coordinated situated of apparatuses for recording client necessities, designing qualities that fulfill these client requirements, and determining any exchange-offs that may be important between the building attributes. Numerous meanings of QFD have been proposed which reflects its numerous features. Be that QFD is fundamentally an individual's framework. Nothing happens without individuals. Its purpose of takeoff is the 'voice of the clients' (VOC). It likewise unites multifunctional groups to cooperate towards fulfilling the client. QFD additionally serves to assemble an organization in the middle of clients and suppliers. Organizations are now and again excessively inside-centered and, consequently, create products or administrations with an ambiguous understanding of the clients' prerequisites, or they are excessively remotely centered, attempting to always satisfy the client at the cost of their own business survival. QFD can help organizations make the key exchange-offs between what the client needs and what the organization can bear to assemble. By focusing endeavors on what will fulfill the clients and the organization most, less time will be used on upgradation and adjustment of the product/ process. It helps organizations to move from an investigation-based methodology to outlining quality into products and as being what is indicated assumes a key part in any aggregate quality administration (TQM) or consistent change system or usage. QFD does nothing that individuals did not do in the recent past, yet it replaces conflicting, natural-choice making processes with an organized methodology.

Numerous organizations rely on their guarantee programs, client grumblings, and inputs from their deals staff to keep them in contact with their clients (Akao, 1990). The result is a concentrate on what is not right with the current product or administration, with almost no consideration on what is correct or what the client truly needs.

The accomplishment of a product or administration generally relies on how they help and desire. Thus, more exertion is included in getting the data important for finding out what the client really needs. This has a tendency to build the introductory arranging time in the undertaking definition period of the advancement cycle, however it diminishes the general process duration in offering a product for sale to the public. One process-situated outline system built to complete the interpretation process and verify that the discoveries are actualized is quality capacity arrangement. QFD is a visual connective process that helps groups concentrate on the needs of the clients all through the aggregate advancement cycle. It gives the ingredients to making an interpretation of client needs into fitting specialized prerequisites for each phase of a product/process development life-cycle.

3

RESEARCH DESIGN FOR MODEL FRAMEWORK

There has been a lot of researches in the direction of improving the efficiency of a manufacturing unit and reducing the cost of production using different techniques like Lean manufacturing, six sigma, reengineering, theory of constraints these researches mainly aim at improving the efficiency of a manufacturing firm by improving the technical aspects of production, like processes, techniques etc. But till today, no research has been found which can find the impact of innovations, use of SPC, right use of scientific methods on costings and, very interestingly, team effectiveness and organizational culture on the costing of a manufacturing unit. This book, apart from looking at SPC and its applications, also aims at establishing the relationship between the positivity in the organizational and productivity and performance and also costing with special reference to the manufacturing units.

RESEARCH OBJECTIVE

The main purpose of the study was to prepare a framework in order to optimize the costing of manufacturing using innovations, SPCs, right use of scientific methods and by improving team effectiveness and organizational culture to enhance productivity and minimize costing of manufacturing. In team effectiveness and organizational culture, the research mainly focused on human as a factor of productivity. It focused on parameters like openness, confrontation, trust etc. and also other characteristics of a team, and determine to what extent these factors can affect the productivity, performance and, thus, the costing of an organization.

RESEARCH DESIGN

Research needs a design or a structure before data collection or analysis can commence. A research design is not just a work plan. The function of a research design is to ensure that the evidence obtained enables us to answer the initial question as unambiguously as possible. Both exploratory and descriptive research were used in the study to identify the problem areas, analyze those problems and then to find solution to those problems. Subsequent to establishing a paradigm, the development of an appropriate research design was pursued. A research design, which is a function of the research objectives, is defined as, "a set of advance decisions that makes up the master plan specifying the methods and procedures for collecting and analyzing the needed information", according to Burns and Bush (2002). An appropriate research design is essential as it determines the type of data, data collection technique, the sampling methodology, the schedule and the budget, according to Hair *et al.* (2003).

There are many frameworks of research design and they can be classified into three traditional categories: exploratory, descriptive and causal (Aaker *et al.*, 2000; Burns and Bush, 2002, Churchill and Iacobucci, 2004, and Hair *et al.*, 2003). Although not compulsory, it is common that researchers utilize multiple research designs (Burns and Bush, 2002), i.e., a researcher may begin with an exploratory study, which will provide the essential background information needed preceding a descriptive study. In turn, the information obtained from a descriptive study may help the researcher design a causal experiment. Exploratory research is conducted to develop initial insights and to provide direction for any further research needed (Malhotra, 2010 and Parasuraman, 1991). It is the foundation of a good study (Churchill and Iacobuci, 2004) and it is normally flexible, unstructured and qualitative (Aaker *et al.*, 2000, Burns and Bush, 2002) and serves as an input to further research (Malhotra, 2010).

An exploratory study is essential when a researcher needs to define the problem more precisely and identify any specific objectives or data requirements to be addressed through an additional research.

As many researchers have noted, descriptive research designs are mostly quantitative in nature (Burns and Bush, 2002, Churchill and Iacobucci, 2004, Hair *et al.*, 2003, and Parasuraman, 1991). There are two basic techniques of descriptive research: cross-sectional and longitudinal. Cross-sectional studies collect information from a given sample of the population at only one point in time, while the latter deals with the same sample units of the population over a period of time (Burns and Bush, 2002) and Malhotra, 2010).

Subsequent to the descriptive study, a causal research was conducted. Descriptive studies may show that two variables are related but are insufficient for examining the cause and effect relationships (Malhotra, 2010). Causal research is most appropriate when the functional relationship between the causal factors and the effect, predicted on the marketing performance variable, is under investigation (Hair *et al.*, 2003).

INSTRUMENT DEVELOPMENT

In this study, a survey was used as the method of primary data collection for the factor team effectiveness and organization culture. The decision to choose a survey method may be based on a number of factors which include sampling, type of population, question form, question content, response rate, costs, and duration of data collection (Aaker *et al.*, 2000). To develop an instrument, the following points are kept in the researchers' mind: measurement scale, content and wording, response format, sequence, physical layout, prepare final draft, revise and finalize.

Three types of measurement scales were used in this research: nominal, ordinal and interval. In relation to the number of scale points, there is no clear rule to indicate an ideal number. Regarding the question content and wording, the questions were designed to be short, simple and comprehensible, avoiding ambiguous, vague, estimation, generalization, and leading, double barreled and presumptuous questions.

The required sample size depends on factors such as the proposed data analysis techniques, financial and access to sampling frame (Malhotra, 2010). As a general rule of thumb, at least 300 cases are deemed comfortable and 500 as very good (Comrey and Lee, 1992, Tabachnick & Fidell, 2001). Thus, it was decided to target a total of 400 respondents from the three sectors mentioned above.

DATA COLLECTION AND ANALYSIS STRATEGY

Data analysis involved steps such as coding the responses, cleaning, screening the data and selecting the appropriate data analysis strategy. The coding task involved identifying, classifying and assigning a numeric or character symbol to the data, which is done in two ways: pre-coded and post-coded.

In this study, all the responses were pre-coded. The process of cleaning and screening data included inconsistency checks and missing responses. All the responses were cleaned and screened and upon completion, the data was then entered to a statistical analysis software package, SPSS for the data analysis.

The final step was to select the appropriate statistical analysis technique. To do this, research elements, namely, the research problem, objectives, characteristics of data and the underlying properties of the statistical techniques are considered. To meet the purposes of this study, exploratory analysis, descriptive analyses, inferential associative and predictive analysis were applied.

ETHICAL CONSIDERATIONS

All participants were made aware of the research intentions and designs through an introduction. The findings have been treated with the utmost confidentiality. No source, whether individual or organization was or will be correlated with specific findings or comment attributed without the express permission of the originator or organization. All discussions will remain confidential in relation to other organizational participants and during the reporting of findings. All participants have the right to anonymity. It was made clear to the participants that they had the right to decline to respond to any question. Participants were treated with utmost respect and their right not to answer a question or withdraw from participation was appreciated. In order not to intrude on privacy, no further efforts were made to contact a potential participant after two attempts. Other than the offer of a copy of the completed dissertation for agreeing to participate, no other participation inducements were offered.

Primary data was collected with an awareness to remain objective and no data was invented. Regarding secondary data sources, all secondary data sources are given full credit for their contribution to this study. The collected data is represented honestly and the analysis is to the best of the author's experience and ability.

CONCLUSION

This study shares some of positivism aspects which recognize only facts and observable phenomena and follow a deductive theory. Under positivism, theories provide the basis of explanation, permit the anticipation of phenomena, predict their occurrence and, therefore, allow them to be controlled (Collis and Hussey, 2009). Explanation consists of establishing causal relationships between the variables by establishing causal laws and linking them to a deductive or integrated theory (Collis and Hussey, 2009). Since it is assumed that social phenomena can be measured, the study was associated with quantitative methods of analysis.

This study followed deductive research approach where theory and hypotheses were developed and a research strategy is designed to test the hypotheses. The study moved from theory to data explaining causal relationships between variables. The study was based on quantitative data analysis, where deductive research approach was most suitable.

4

IMPACT OF STATISTICAL PROCESS CONTROL

We have briefly discussed SPC and its scope for application in Chapter 1. These days, statistical techniques act as a supportive tool for the representation and analysis of measurement data. The industrial standards and guidelines recommend utilization of different statistical techniques for successful process management. Among all the statistical techniques, the interest to apply SPC techniques in the industry has also been growing exponentially during the last decade, as organizations advance in maturity levels within the frameworks of process improvement models, such as Capability Maturity Model (CMM, Paulk, M.C. *et al.*, 1993), Capability Maturity Model Integration (CMMI, Product Team, 2001) and Software Process Improvement and Capability Determination (SPICE, ISO/IEC 15504 - 4 and 5, 1998). These models implicitly direct different companies to implement SPC as a vital step for achieving higher process maturity levels. They suggest control charts for both project-level process control and organizational-level process improvement purposes. Many researchers contribute to this trend by providing approaches to utilize the SPC techniques for the manufacturing industry (Burr, A. *et al.*, 1993, Florac, A.W. *et al.* (a), (b), (c) and (d), 1999, and Carleton, A., 2001). SPC is a powerful tool to optimize the amount of information needed for use in making management decisions. It also provides an understanding of the business baselines, insights for process improvements, communication of value and results of processes. SPC provides real-time analysis to establish controllable process baselines; learn, set, and dynamically improve process capabilities; and focus on business areas needing improvement.

MANUFACTURING PROCESS

Manufacturing Process, as we know it today, started in first quarter of the 18th century. Ever since, many theories, procedures and systems have been developed to get the best results out of the process. There has been a constantly increasing pressure exerted by the human society to reduce cost and standardize the quality.

A huge compendium of work has been done already. After a extensive research – both with respect to the industry as well as academically – ISO 9001, QS 9000, ISO/TS 16949, 2008 and ISO 14001 systems, over 175 white papers, over 50 books, 3 Ph.D., many research papers, over 200 scientific experiments, 4 innovations and 5 experiments were found to done before this research. The way manufacturing can be understood by a common man's point of view will be, "Converting one or more materials into a simple or assembled product which can be used by him." Thus, if a simple product – refrigerator – is taken, the manufacturing will involve broadly three main categories, namely, prime ingredients, assembly equipment and assembly line.

Prime Ingredients

- **Steel/Metal Parts:** These are primarily used to make the outer body of the refrigerator, which helps to define the shape and volume of the product.
- **Electrical Parts:** These are the parts which make the refrigerator perform, and these may range from simple motors to complex compressors.
- **Plastic Parts and Glass:** These are used to define the storage space within the product.

Assembly equipment

- Zigs and Fixtures
- Torque Screw Drivers, Screws, Nuts, Bolts, etc
- Wires and Cables

Assembly line

- Assembly Tables and Conveyer Belts
- Robots/Manpower

As we understand from the above, it is not complete list but a demonstrative list. But it makes clear that every step needs some sort of production activity and thus human involvement as well. This makes it very clear that when we talk about manufacturing and making it work smoothly, the following four factors are of utmost importance:

- Proper Application of Principles of Physics
- Proper Implementation of Standards like ISO, ISO/TS, 5S, 3R, Lean Manufacturing, etc.
- Innovativeness
- Man Power Handling

Almost all manufacturing is done before starting and going for 'batch production' or 'mass production', with a hit-and-trial process to achieve the results. In almost all cases, this becomes the standard benchmark for how to produce the 'product'. Today, as we work and spread our vision, companies, due to rising pressure on the cost, are working day and night to make their process leaner. The theory today making inroads in a big way is 'any process not adding value is a waste and thus should not be present'.

A big misconception is that 'automation is the solution'. Yes it is but not yet true. Irrespective of the level of automation, we still have a human being at the helm of affairs. Not only this, but there are many a complex operations which only a human brain can tackle. Examples for this can be seen at Ford Motors' Chicago plant, Rolls Royce's Bristol (UK) plant and many such plants, where the process is governed heavily by people – may it be assembly or fitment.

SPC APPLICATION

SPC is a methodology that aims to provide process control in statistical terms (Sutherland, J. *et al.*, 1992). SPC has been widely used in manufacturing industries in order to control variability and improve processes. W. A. Shewart (1939) was working on the idea of quality control and he brought the idea that each process is driven by forces of variation. According to Shewart (1939), variation in a process has two types of causes: assignable causes and chance causes. (Deming (2000) refers them as 'common causes'). Assignable causes appear in unexpected periods and can be fixed by immediate actions. For instance, if a new tool is being used for coding, the productivity of the coder may be lower during the adaptation period.

SPC is used to describe the variability that can be controlled or that which cannot be controlled. This variability is also called common cause or special cause. Common cause occurs with the nature of the process. It exists in all processes and it is the variability from the system. Special cause is not the part of the process. It exists in almost all processes because of certain reasons. If there is no variability because of special causes, it means that the process is statistically under control. For a process that is statistically under control, the researcher can conclude that it has a definable identification and a definable capability. In a process that is under control, by removing all special causes that are noticed until then, the remaining variability would come from common causes. After taking the process under control, the next stage improves the process.

The only target for the production is to get the s control, and to reduce the variables in the same time. Because, as the variables reduce, the costs reduce too. The key steps for implementing SPC are: (a) identify defined processes, (b) identify measurable attributes of the process, (c) characterize natural variation of attributes and (d) track the process variation. If the process is in control, continue to track and if the process is not in control then (a) identify assignable cause, (b) remove assignable cause and (c) finally return to track the process variation.

SPC Tools

SPC aims to produce the products in the most economic and useful way using statistical principles and techniques at every stage of the production. In this manner, SPC aims faithfulness to the standards and provides the fitness of the specifications that have been determined earlier. It is used to reduce the defect products as much as possible. SPC is a powerful collection of problem-solving tools useful in achieving process stability and improving capability through the reduction of variability. These tools (Table 4.1), often called the 'magnificent seven' (Montgomery, D.C., 1991 and Paulk, M.C., 2000) are Check Sheet, Histogram, Pareto Chart, Cause-and-Effect Diagram, Scatter Diagram, Control Chart and Graph.

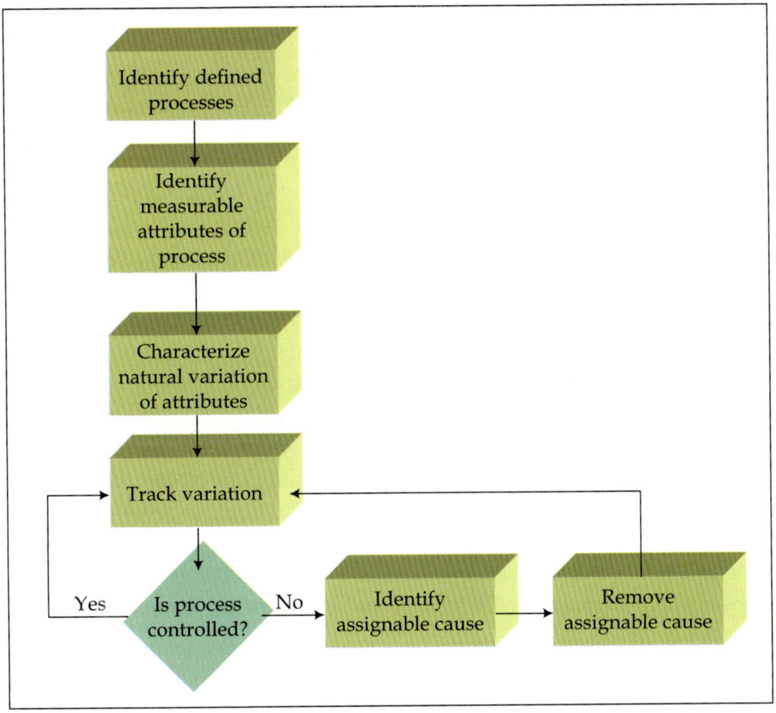

Fig. 4.1 How to Perform Statistical Process Control

Table 4.1 The Seven Tools and Their Example of Use

Tool	Application
Check Sheet	To count occurrences of problems
Histogram	To identify central tendencies and any skewing to one side or the other
Pareto Chart	To identify the 20% of the modules which yield 80% of the issues
Cause and Effect Diagram	To identify assignable causes
Scatter Diagram	To identify correlation and suggest causation
Control Chart	To identify processes that are out of control
Graph	To use for visual data, e.g., in a pie chart.

Application Study

In this study, the weight of product in food sector was examined. The upper specification limit of the product was 200 g and the lower specification limit was 194 g. In the packing process 25 samples were drawn. All samples included five packets. The X and S charts were constructed for the sample in question. Mean and standard deviation control charts showed that, the deviations, in mean and distribution were not out of 3-sigma limits for the process characteristic of interest. The mean for the sample was 206.8, but the upper specification limit was 200. So, the mean was larger than the specification limit. The expected mean was 197, but the mean for the sample was 206.8. That means the packets were filled more than they should have been. The calculated standard deviation, 3.863, was much more than expected standard deviation 0.75. Therefore, the variability was bigger than expected. Six points in a row were above the centerline in the control charts.

Process Improvements

Proper SPC starts with planning and data collection. Statistical analysis on the wrong or incorrect data is rubbish. The analysis must be appropriate for the data collected. Be sure to **plan** – then constantly re-evaluate your situation to make sure that the plan is correct.

The key to any process improvement program is the PDSA cycle, described by Walter Shewart, which is given below.

- **Plan:** Identify the problem and the possible causes. The quality control tools described in this book can help organizations identify problems and possible causes, and to prioritize corrective actions.
- **Do:** Make changes designed to correct or improve the situation.
- **Study:** Study the effect of these changes on the situation. This is where, control charts are used. They show the effects of changes on a process over time. Evaluate the results and then replicate the change, or abandon it and try something different.
- **Act:** If the result is successful, standardize the changes and then work on further improvements for the next prioritized problem. If the outcome is not yet successful, look for other ways to change the process or identify different causes for the problem. Control charting is one of a number of steps involved in SPC. The steps include discovery, analysis, prioritization, clarification, and then charting. Before using the statistical QC software, appropriate data must be collected for analysis. Then, you need to begin again and do it over and over and over... Remember, quality is a cycle of continuous improvement.

Application Areas of SPC

SPC is an analytical decision-making tool which allows you to see when a process is working correctly and when it is not. Variation is present in any process – deciding when the variation is natural and when it needs correction is the key to quality control. As we have discussed earlier, the foundation for SPC was laid by Dr. Walter Shewart, working in the Bell Telephone Laboratories in the 1920s, conducting research on methods to improve quality and lower costs. He developed the concept of 'control' with regard to variation, and came up with SPC charts which provide a simple way to determine if the process is in control or not. Dr. W. Edwards Deming built upon Shewart's work and took the concepts to Japan following WWII. There, the Japanese industry adopted the concepts whole-heartedly. The resulting high quality of the Japanese products is world-renowned. Dr. Deming is famous throughout Japan as a 'God of quality'. Table 4.2 shows the application areas of SPC.

Table 4.2 The Application Areas of SPC

SPC Technique	Application	Process/Attributes	Discussion/Results	Reference
Control Chart	Military software unit maintaining almost 380,000 source lines of code	Defects per person-day and defects per thousand lines of code.	SPC techniques introduced along with software engineering project management techniques, inspections, and metrics. Process improvement resulted in 20% more code being produced than on the previous version.	(French, 1995)
X Control Chart	Process automation and consumer electronics projects in C++, ranging from 150 to 400 function points	Defects per thousand lines of code for code review and testing. Lines of code per hour for inspection preparation.	Illustrates how using control charts identified out-of-control processes. Corrective actions were implemented to remove assignable causes.	(Jacob and Pillai, 2003)
XmR Control Chart	GCOS 8 (an operating system)	Inspection review rate and defect-detection effectiveness of software inspections.	Identified sub processes (inspections of new code and revised code). Demonstrated inspections were under control. Estimated defects remaining in the code.	(Weller, 2000)
XmR Control Chart and u-Chart	Space Shuttle Onboard Software	Inspection review rate, defect-detected in inspections and test.	Trial study of SPC. Identified inspection sub processes and natural variation of these processes.	(Florac, et. al., 2000)

Z-Chart	A sample of 298 engineers training in the Software Engineering Institute's Personal Software Process (PSP)	Defects discovered in design reviews.	Process control charts presented in the context of metrics collected by engineers going through PSP training. Demonstrations of the effectiveness of the PSP based on size estimation accuracy, effort estimation accuracy, defects per source line remove early in the lifecycle, and productivity.	(Hayes, 1998)
Confidence intervals based on statistical models of failures	Ericsson Lab, Italy	Effectiveness in failure detection of function testing.	Pilot study. Concluded process control for function test can be based on examined models.	(Bertolino, et. al., 2002)
Regression model, Outlier analysis, Box plot	Large Y2K maintenance project. Part of a major international software enterprise in Caserta, Italy.	Size and productivity metrics during maintenance.	Study analyzed correlation, characterized patterns of variations, developed regression model to predict impact of maintenance. Concluded that the maintenance process is predictable, repeatable, and suitable for SPC.	(De Lucia, et. al., 2002)

Implementing Issues of SPC

The implementing issues of SPC are shown in Table 4.3 below:

Table 4.3 Implementing Issues of SPCA (Card, 1994)

Define the Process	Consistent measurements cannot be expected from software processes that are not documented and generally followed.
Choose Appropriate Measures	Measures need not be exhaustive. One or two measures that provide insight into the performance of a process or activity are adequate, especially if the measures are related to the process or activity goal. Measures that can be tracked inexpensively are preferable.
Focus on the Process Trends	Control charts should be constructed so as to detect process trends, not individual non-conforming events.
Calculate the Control Limits Correctly	Straightforward formulas exist for calculating control limits and analyzing distributions. Introductory college courses in statistics usually do not address process-control techniques in detail.
Investigate and Act	SPC only signals the possible existence of a problem. Without detailed investigations, as in an audit, and instituting corrective action, SPC will not provide any benefit.
Provide Training	Problems in following the above recommendations for implementing SPC can be decreased with effective training. SPC training based on examples of software processes is preferred.

CONCLUSION

SPC has gained importance in recent years for providing process control and achieving higher production. In spite of importance of SPC, there are very few resources that describe implementation details and guidelines while applying SPC to the specific processes. The complexity of the processes and the existence of too many parameters for the process control raise variability and make it difficult to apply SPC to quality production. But, still it is an effective tool as it provides a visual interface with a scientific foundation. For this reason, companies are trying to use SPC techniques as they mature their processes. It is not easy, but with more experience and trials, better outcomes can be obtained from SPC.

5

IMPACT OF ORGANIZATIONAL CULTURE

In recent years, quality manufacturing is growing in an exponential manner. Quality manufacturing plays a very important role in the success of a manufacturing unit. These units measure their performance in the terms of quality and reliability manufacturing of its products. For this purpose, manufacturing should follow quality models, guidelines, six sigma as well as employees' technical skills. The perception of employees is also important for high quality output. Perceptions of work conditions have proven to be important for the well-being of workers. Teamwork is the key for efficient production. The teamwork is directly related to the work culture of manufacturing unit(s). It is well known that the profit of any company is correlated with employee attitudes and perceptions of work conditions, but still research in this direction is not has been focused. Therefore, we identified the various issues related to employees and work culture, and then established the relationship among them.

INTRODUCTION

Manufacturing is a crucial component of the foundation that maintains the security, health, and wealth of any country. Quality manufacturing plays key role in terms of factory performance. One of the most important measure to determine the factory performance is the 'factory cycle time', which means delivering the right product, at the right place and at the right time. These days, the performance measure of the manufacturing units (load-adjusted cycle-time efficiency) remains more or less the same as it was half a century ago. Although the goods produced in the factories have evolved in terms of sophistication, reliability, the time spent in their complete production remains almost the same with only 5-20% decrement. Due to this reason, there is enormous scope for improvement in the running of almost any manufacturing unit in any country. Lean manufacturing, six sigma, reengineering, theory of constraint are the works done previously in this field which can improve the performance of any manufacturing unit when and if applied properly. These techniques are mostly related to the technical aspects of production. One another aspect of production which is responsible for the success of any organization is the 'human factor', without which no software is of any use, and no machine would even work. The success of any business depends on appropriate, effective, well-communicated, HR and business practices, where the importance of team effectiveness and organizational culture cannot be neglected. We focused our attention to find out how team effectiveness and positive organizational culture could affect the cost and productivity of any manufacturing unit. So a relationship between the performance of the employees and organizational culture was established. We showed that organizational culture has an impact on productivity and costing of any manufacturing unit and, for this purpose, two HR tools viz. Team Effectiveness Assessment Measure (TEAM) and OCTAPACE was used (O - Openness and Risk Taking, C – Confrontation, T - Trust, A-Authenticity, P – Pro-activity, A – Autonomy, C – Collaboration, E – Experimenting). The TEAM was used for assessing the team effectiveness in the organization while OCTAPACE was used for assessing the organizational culture.

SOME MILESTONE RESEARCHES

The viewpoint of Beeman, Don R. Sharkey, Thomas W (1987) brought into sharp focus that one of the most difficult circumstances for a manager is to be suddenly transported into a significant position in a highly politicized organization. In a very short time, the manager will be wondering whether such a situation can be anything except a no-win situation. This chapter explains the foundations of political behavior, identifies highly political situations, and provides the new manager with the tools to deal with negative political behaviors. A new manager is in a situation, when entering a new job, with high levels of complexity and competition. One of the first assessments the new manager must make is the intensity of the political behavior in the new organization.

M. Brunett, C. Cook and G. Rothermel (2004) described that, today, the end-user programming has become the most common form of programming, but still there has been little investigation into the dependability of the programs the end users create. This is of critical importance and can be problematic because the dependability of these programs are very important, as in certain cases, errors in end-user programs, such as errors in formulae in spreadsheets, can have costs of millions of dollars attached. So, in this situation, this problem is dealt by developing a software-engineering paradigm viable for the end-user programming, an approach called end-user software engineering.

The authors R.Y. Chang, A. Podgurski and J. Yang (2007) described that neglected conditions are an important but difficult-to-find class of software defects. This chapter presents an approach to reveal the neglected conditions that integrates static program analysis and advanced data mining techniques to discover implicit conditional rules in a code base and to discover rule violations that indicate neglected conditions. In this approach, the user is required to indicate minimal constraints on the context of the rules to be sought, rather than specific rule templates, and to permit this generality, rules are modeled as graph 'minors' of program dependence graphs, and both frequent item set mining and frequent sub-graph mining algorithms are employed to identify candidate rules. The results are reported, of an empirical evaluation of the approach in which it was used to discover conditional rules and neglect conditions in ~25,000 lines of source code.

According to Shen-Wen Cheng (2008), in today's scenario, the systems must have the ability to self-adapt to the changes in their environment. But the existing systems require human oversight or are limited in the kinds of system and set of quality-of-service concerns they address. This approach uses software architecture models and architectural styles to overcome the limitations of the existing systems. The target system and its environment is monitored by the engineering approach and framework of mechanism provided by the approach. It reflects the observations into a system's architectural model detect scope of improvement select a course of action and effect the changes in a close loop. The infrastructure provided is general and reusable with well-defined customization, which allows the engineers to systematically customize the approach to particular systems and concerns. Some concepts are referenced from Goodman et al. (1986 and 1987), Parker (1990 and 1994), Orsburn (1990), Fisher, K. (1993), and Stevens, (1994).

Research Objective

The main purpose of the study was to study the relationship between the organizational culture and the productivity and costing of a manufacturing unit. The research mainly focused on human as a factor of productivity. The study focused on parameters like openness, confrontation, trust etc. and other characteristics of a team as well, and determined to what extent these factors could affect the productivity, performance and thus costing of an organization.

Specifically, the *objectives* of the present work were:

- To study how the culture of an organization affected the costing of a manufacturing firm.
- To study how the organizational culture affected the productivity of a manufacturing firm.

Rationale for research

There has been a lot of researches in the direction of improving the efficiency of a manufacturing unit and reducing the cost of production using different techniques, like lean manufacturing, six sigma, reengineering, theory of constraints and so on. These researches mainly aim at improving the efficiency of a manufacturing firm by improving the technical aspects of production, like processes, techniques etc., but, till date, very little research has been undertaken which can relate team effectiveness and organizational culture with the costing of a manufacturing unit. Our research aimed at establishing the relationship between the positivity in the organizational and productivity and performance and, also, costing, with special reference to manufacturing units.

Research Method Deployed

Here let us discuss about the research methodology which was used in this research project, establishing a framework for collection, analysis and interpretation of primary and secondary data.

Research design

Research needs a design or a structure before data collection or analysis can commence. A research design is not just a work plan. The function of a research design is to ensure that the evidence obtained enables us to answer the initial question as unambiguously as possible. Both exploratory and descriptive research were used in this project to identify the problem areas, analyze those problems and then to find solution to those problems.

Research question

Issues related to how team-effectiveness and organizational culture can affect the productivity and, thus, the costing of an organization, is a matter of debate all across the world. To what extent can efforts be made towards improving the teams and making organizational culture increase the efficiency of the organizations and how much is it worthwhile to spend money and resources in this area is still a big question. Against this background, following questions were framed:

- What impact does team effectiveness has on the costing and productivity of a manufacturing unit?
- Can culture of an organization have an impact on the costing and productivity of a manufacturing unit?

Data collection procedures

Keeping in view the attributes of the sample chosen by us, the data was collected by structured questionnaire and interviews. Respondents were approached personally and were requested to provide the required details. Questionnaires were also filled by getting the required information if the respondent did not have time to fill it. The respondents were interviewed personally using OCTAPACE and were asked to rate their organization according to their perception based on the parameters given in the questionnaire.

Data analysis

Data analysis and interpretation tools and techniques were decided keeping in view the nature and type of data collected. So in our research, IBM SPSS 19.0 and Microsoft Excel were used for the analysis of data.

Hypothesis testing

Hypothesis is used to establish whether the difference exhibited by random samples can be inferred to the population from which the samples have originated.

(i) **Null hypothesis:** There was no correlation between costing and productivity of manufacturing units and the organizational culture.

(ii) **Alternative hypothesis:** There was a correlation between the costing and productivity of manufacturing units and team-effectiveness and organizational culture.

Correlation results

The correlation between performance and various dependent attributes was analyzed (Fig. 5.1). The dependent attributes were interaction amongst employees, genuine sharing of information and feelings in a meeting, free discussion and communication and discussion between seniors and subordinates, analysis of interpersonal problems, the tendency of passing the buck on others when there was a problem, tendency to let the problem surface, interpersonal contact and support among employees, tendency to confide in seniors, tendency of team members to fend themselves when there was a problem, congruity between feelings, tactfulness, tendency to owe up mistakes, encouragement of subordinates, tendency of consideration, prevention is better than cure, supervision of employee, tendency of subordinates, the feeling of team work, the tendency to accept, employee's involvement in developing organizational mission and goals, the tendency of employees, performance and thinking, performance and experimentation.

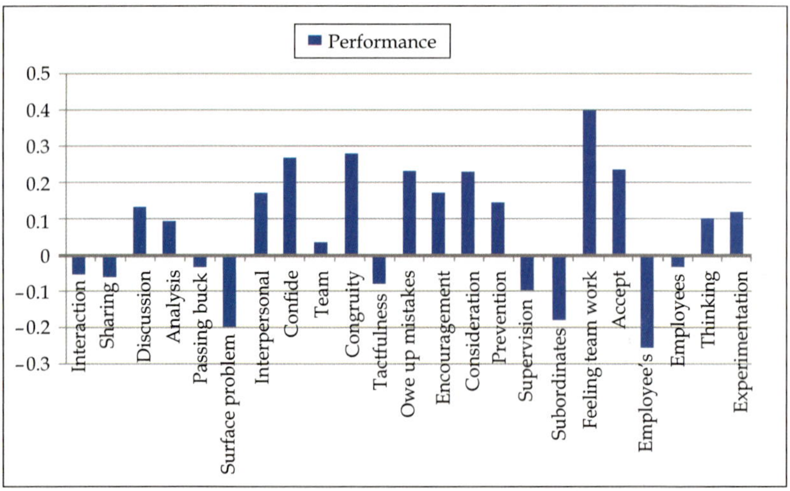

Fig. 5.1 Correlation between Performance and Dependent Variables

Result for hypothesis

The null hypothesis was, "There is no correlation between costing of manufacturing units and team-effectiveness and organizational culture", but results showed that the team-effectiveness and organizational culture have relationship with the performance of any manufacturing unit, thus indirectly it also has a relationship with the costing of manufacturing units. So, the null hypothesis was rejected.

KEY FINDINGS

- Free interaction amongst the employees decreased the performance of the team. Managers at different levels didn't want their subordinates to interact much at the work place.
- Employees believed that if they genuinely share thoughts and feelings in meetings, it would negatively affect their performance. They were reluctant in sharing feelings with each other and specially their seniors in the meetings.
- Free discussion and communication was considered to be vital for the performance of an organization. Employees wanted a culture of free discussion and communication in their organization.
- Deep analysis of problems was considered to be vital for good and consistent performance in the long run. In general, the employees were of the opinion that if the problems were surfaced it would create a problem in future.
- The culture of passing the buck on each other hindered the performance of an organization.
- Interpersonal support and contact among employees is vital for the performance of an organization.
- For the performance of a team in an organization, feeling of trust and confidence between the seniors and the subordinates is very important.
- It was found that employees believed that if the performance is low they will have to fend for themselves.
- People believed that within a team if there is a congruity between expressed behaviors and actual feelings, it would increase the performance of the team.
- People thought that using tactfulness and manipulation for getting things done would adversely affect the performance of a team.

- The culture of owing up mistakes in an organization is vital for the performance of an organization.
- Managers at different levels were of the opinion that too much freedom to their employees to take independent actions relating to their jobs would decrease the performance of their team.
- At the same time, the employees didn't like the tendency of their seniors to over-supervise them and direct them from time to time.
- Employees wanted that they should be given some freedom so as to handle certain problems on their own. They found it useless to check out with their seniors, for every small problem.
- Performance showed highest degree of correlation with team work and team spirit. People believed that team work and team spirit was the most vital thing for the performance of an organization.
- Managers at different level believed that the employees should not be involved in setting organizational goals and missions, as it would decrease the performance of the teams.
- The managers believed that although experimentation and innovation in doing things is important, too much of it would risk the stability of an organization, which would be a threat to the organizations existence in today's competitive world.

CONCLUSIONS

The main points are as follows with respect our work in the Perception of Employees with respect to Impact of Organizational Culture on the Costing and Productivity of a Manufacturing Unit

- Too much of interaction among employees in a manufacturing firm can reduce the performance of the unit. It can thus increase the cost related to time factor and per unit cost due to decreased productivity.
- Employees are afraid to come up openly regarding their true feelings about any problem or issue in front of their seniors in meetings. They tend to manipulate things in the meetings as they feel that frank expression of feelings might become a threat in future. This could result in employees hiding very important facts about low performances of teams or actual potential of a particular team in terms of

productivity and thus the problem may continue to persist for a long time, adversely affecting the profitability.

- If there is a culture of trust and amicability in an organization, the processes flow smoothly, saves time and energy, increases the performance of the teams as well as reduces the cost related to time factor and wastage.
- Greater coordination and effectiveness in teams would result into better productivity due to increase in performance hence greater profitability of the firm. This would further reduce the cost per unit.
- Fixed cost factor can only be overcome with the help higher productivity levels in a manufacturing unit. To realize economies of scale, team work and coordination is of great importance.
- Feeling of trust, confidence and mutual understanding between the seniors and subordinates can increase the profitability of a firm by motivating the employees for higher performance and timely redressing of their grievances which could hinder work flow.
- Giving employees a degree of freedom regarding decision making on their own to some extent may prevent delays in complexities of routine nature.
- The involvement of employees in setting goals and missions of an organization might not prove to be a very wise decision as the employees might seek their own comfort in setting the goals and missions of their organization and neglecting the organizational needs and objectives.

Experimentation and innovation is not always considered good as going by already set rules and methods of solving a problem reduces time required for solving it and also the chances of errors.

6

ENTREPRENEURSHIP AND INNOVATION

ENTREPRENEURSHIP

Internationally, business leaders are engaged in a debate on the key aspects of success in businesses. Goel and Farooque (2014) observed, "Entrepreneurship is essential for economic development. In capitalistic economies, the entrepreneurs played an important role in their development. In socialist economies, the State played the role of the entrepreneur. But in a developing country like India, which followed the path of mixed economy, both the government and the private entrepreneurs played an equally important role." The Union Finance Minister of India, Mr Arun Jaitley stated, while presenting the Union Budget 2015-16, "The Indian economy has turned around dramatically in the last nine months with the real GDP growth expected to accelerate to 7.4%, making India the fastest growing economy in the world." Entrepreneurs, in the post-liberalized period of the Indian economy, have played a pivotal role in developing the country and have emerged as the key drivers of the economy. Goel and Farooque (2014) identified the following characteristics of entrepreneurship:

- It helps the formation of capital by bringing together the savings and investments of people.
- It provides large-scale employment opportunities and increases the purchasing power of the people.
- It promotes balanced regional development in the country.
- It helps reducing the concentration of economic power (power to own the factor of production in few hands).

Derivation of the Term 'Entrepreneurship'

The term 'entrepreneurship' has been assigned varied meanings. National Knowledge Commission (NKC), India stated, "Entrepreneurship is the professional application of knowledge, skills and competencies and/or of monetizing a new idea, by an individual or set of people by launching an enterprise *de novo* or diversifying from an existing one (distinct from seeking self-employment as in profession or trade), thus to pursue growth while generating wealth, employment and social good." An entrepreneur is an individual who operates a new venture and willingly assumes the risks by strategically analyzing the environment. The various obstacles that these entrepreneurs face can be termed as challenges. The successful entrepreneurs are visionaries who saw the direction of the wind as well as the bigger picture. They grew because they started small and remained consistent with their goals. True entrepreneurs are resourceful, passionate and driven to succeed and improve. The term 'entrepreneurship' has come from the French word *entreprendre* and the German word *unternehmen* meaning 'to undertake'. Entrepreneurship refers to the process of initiating a business or any other type of organization. An entrepreneur develops a business plan, acquires human and other required resources, and is entirely responsible for its success or failure. Entrepreneurship operates within an entrepreneurship ecosystem. Thames (2012) quoted Peter Drucker and observed, "Innovation, which is the specific function of entrepreneurship, is the means by which the entrepreneur either creates new wealth-producing resources or endows existing resources with enhanced potential for creating wealth." He further continued that according to Drucker, "...the very foundation of entrepreneurship is the practice of systematic innovation." There are two other critical aspects – entrepreneurial strategies and entrepreneurial management – and both deserve separate discussions.

Role of Entrepreneurs in Developing India

Jain (2011) stated, "Before 1991, Indian business success was a function of ambition, licenses, government contacts, and an understanding of the bureaucratic system. Decisions were based on connections, rather than the market or competition. Business goals reflected a continuation of the *swadeshi* movement, which promoted import substitution to attain economic freedom from the West. Pre-1991 policies were inward looking and geared towards the attainment of self-reliance. During that era, entrepreneurship was subdued, capital was limited and India had very few success stories. Also, the society was risk averse and the individuals were primarily concerned with employment stability."

According to the Global Entrepreneurship Monitor (GEM) Report (2007), India's High-Growth Expectation Early-Stage Entrepreneurship (HEA) rate is only one fifth of that of China. Further, among medium- and low-income countries, China's nascent and new entrepreneurs appear to be the most growth-oriented, with more than 10 per cent of them anticipating high growth. Early-stage entrepreneurial activity in India is marked by low levels of growth expectation. This is despite the extremely high levels of potential entrepreneurial activity as perceived by the non-entrepreneurially active population in the country.

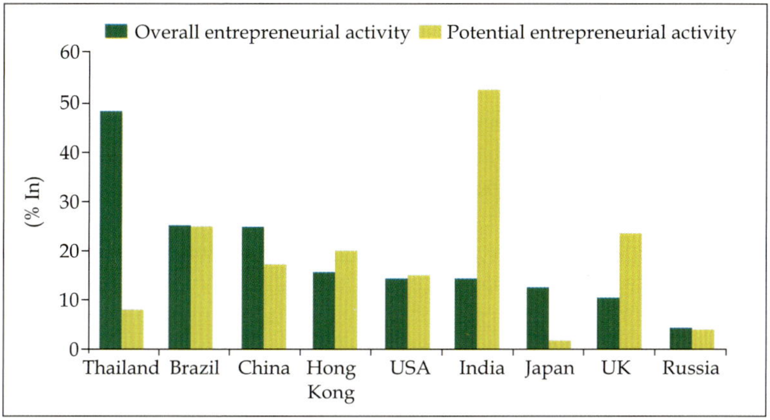

Overall and potential entrepreneurial activity

According to the sixty-second round of National Sample Survey (NSS), in rural India, almost 50 per cent of all workers are self-employed – 57 per cent among males and nearly 62 per cent among females, while the corresponding figures in urban India are 42 for males and 44 for females. The essential feature of the self-employed is that they have autonomy (decide how, where and when to produce) and economic independence (in respect of choice of market, scale of operation and finance) for carrying out their operation. According to GEM Report (2013), "... economies like Jamaica, India and Malawi have close to 40% of necessity-driven early-stage entrepreneurs."

Challenges Faced by Indian Entrepreneurs

Due to globalization, although a plethora of alternatives became available, but these were under intense level of competition. Initially, it had been observed that for the old business houses success was derived from closely-knit joint-family structures which fostered teamwork, family values, and tenacity of purpose. These aspects were definitely present, but the method of doing business has changed radically with the times. Kanchana *et al.* (2013) opined, "The most important challenges faced by entrepreneurs today included developing the vision and business idea, raising capital for a startup, assembling a business team, finding the right business location, finding right set of employees, finding good customers, dealing with competition, unforeseen business challenges and expenses, keeping up with industrial changes and trends, lack of support, negative mindset, lack of marketing facilities, lack of infrastructural facilities etc. So it is necessary to overcome these challenges in order to conduct an efficient business."

Shortage of skills is another challenge which requires due attention. *Business Today* (March 31, 2013) reports, 'While attitudes are beginning to change in a small way, evidence suggests that young people still see little value in vocational education or skill development programs. A recent McKinsey report covering 8,500 respondents in nine countries, titled *Education to Employment*, notes that only 21 per cent of young Indians felt that education beyond the secondary level – whether vocational or academic – would not add value to their lives. Sixty-four per cent say a conventional education is more valued by the society.

INNOVATION MANAGEMENT

Innovation management is focused on the systematic processes that organizations use to develop new and improved products, services and business processes. It involves harnessing the creative ideas of an organization's employees and utilizing it to bring a steady pipeline of profitable new innovations to the marketplace, quickly and efficiently.

Innovation management is the discipline of managing processes in innovation. It can be used to develop both product and organizational innovation. Without proper processes, it is not possible for R&D to be efficient. Innovation management includes a set of tools that allow managers and engineers to cooperate with a common understanding of goals and processes. The focus of innovation management is to allow the organization to respond to an external or internal opportunity, and use its creative efforts to introduce new ideas, processes or products. Given below is a brief description of some of the key characteristics of innovation management.

- Importantly, innovation management is not relegated to R&D. It involves workers at every level in contributing creatively to a company's development, manufacturing, and marketing. By utilizing appropriate innovation management tools, the management can trigger and deploy the creative juices of the whole workforce towards the continuous development of a company.
- The process can be viewed as an evolutionary integration of organization, technology and market by iterating a series of activities – search, select, implement and capture.
- Innovation processes can either be pushed or pulled through development. A pushed process is based on an existing or a newly invented technology that the organization has access to, and tries to find profitable applications to use this technology. A pulled process tries to find areas where customers' needs are not met, and then focus development efforts to find solutions to those needs.
- To succeed with either method, an understanding of both the market and the technical problems are needed. By creating multi-functional development teams, containing engineers and marketers, both the dimensions can be solved.
- The lifetime (or product lifecycle) of new products is steadily getting shorter. Increased competition therefore forces companies reduce the time to market. Innovation managers must therefore decrease development time, without sacrificing quality or meeting the needs of the market.

Common tools include brainstorming, virtual prototyping, product-lifecycle management, idea management, Theory of Inventive Problem Solving or TRIZ, stage-gate process, project management, product-line planning and portfolio management.

Managing Complex Innovation

To manage complex innovation, one must ask the right questions. Innovation is the change that outperforms the previous practice. To lead or sustain with innovations, managers need to concentrate heavily on the innovation network which requires deep understanding of the complexity of innovation. Collaboration is an important source of innovation. Innovations are increasingly brought to the market by networks of firms, selected according to their comparative advantages, and operating in a coordinated manner. When a technology goes through a major transformational phase and yields a successful innovation, then it becomes a great learning experience not only for the parent industry but also for other industries as well. Big innovations are generally the outcome of intra- and interdisciplinary networking among technological sectors, along with combination of implicit and explicit knowledge.

Five basic steps to follow when you want to develop new products and services that actually become success are:

Aim high

Strive for disruptive, rather than incremental, innovation. Incremental innovation focuses on making small improvements to existing products and services. It adds a few new bells and whistles, but does not significantly alter the product or the perceived value to the customer. Disruptive innovation creates new products or services that solve customer problems in entirely new and different ways. It fundamentally alters the customer's perception of value, and can literally turn markets and entire industries upside down. Often, disruptive innovation solves problems that customers didn't know they had or were unable to clearly articulate. Incremental innovation generally costs less and is easier to achieve. But it rarely leads to a position of market leadership. Disruptive innovation takes longer, costs more, and has a much higher failure rate. But when successful, the payoff is huge.

Get your customers involved

A recent study of future mobile phone services compared new product ideas from customers with those put forth by 'internal' sources – professional developers and technology experts. Researchers found that the internal experts come up with more new product ideas that had a good chance of actually making it to the market. However, customers created more new product ideas that actually solved their problems, which were a major factor in determining the perceived value. Getting customers involved in the creative/idea generation phase of your innovation process may take longer and cost more. But it greatly increases the odds of developing successful new products. It also keeps you in touch with the problems which your customers face, which can change a lot faster than you think. Your customers represent a bountiful source of new product ideas, and the process of engaging them is likely to produce other benefits like stronger working relationships and deeper loyalty as well.

Manage the process

Many people think that in order to successfully innovate, all you have to do is to come up with a bunch of creative ideas. Not so. To reap the desired rewards, innovation must be carefully managed from the beginning to the end. It starts with idea generation, followed closely by idea evaluation and then implementation. Creativity doesn't become innovation until you actually bring a new product or service to market that customers are willing to pay for.

Build a culture that supports innovation

To succeed, the innovation needs to become an integral part of how you do business. It must be an ongoing process in which you never stop looking for new and better ways to add value. And that requires a culture that supports innovation for a longer term. Get in the habit of constantly challenging your assumptions about your business, your market and your industry so that you do not get stuck in "that's the way we've always done it around here." Teach your people to think differently so that they can see the world in new and different ways. Show employees how and where they fit into the innovation process. Ask for their ideas on how to improve products, processes and workflow, and keep the lines of communication open – up and down the organization.

Look outside the box

For most companies, innovation remains an internal process. Ideas are generated, developed, and brought to market using the talents, skills and resources that reside within the organization. In a world that doesn't change very quickly, this approach will generally produce satisfactory results. But the world moves a lot faster these days, and relying solely on internally generated ideas may mean that faster, more agile competitors will beat you in marketing with new products or services. For this reason, forward-looking companies have begun experimenting with innovation models that combine internal and external resources. Some companies are having success with the 'connect and develop' model, which consists of importing ideas from outside sources and enhancing them internally. Others are 'off-shoring' their R&D centers to put them closer to sources of raw materials, labor and new ideas. Regardless of the model, the idea is that tapping into ideas and resources outside the organization will enable you to bring new products to market faster, cheaper and with a better chance of success. The next generation of market leaders will do more than just brainstorm their way to success. They will aim high, get the customers involved, establish the right culture, and look beyond their borders for new product and service ideas. Most of all, they will manage the innovation process as if their very survival depends on it. In today's markets, that may well be true.

SIMPLE MANTRAS IN ENTREPRENEURSHIP AND INNOVATION

Innovating to Improve Profits

As it is not feasible to write or study every industry or process because of want of space in this book, we will simply take one example and try to improve. We shall start with current costing, steps taken and the improvement achieved. In the end, we will put the steps forward so that the process engineers can think, study and implement. For this, we shall use a simple device, 'Air Dispenser'.

The Product

The product consists of the following elements:

1. Body
2. Plate
3. Cap Body

4. Spindle
5. Foam-57
6. Spring
7. Hex Nut
8. Packaging Cost
9. Assembly Cost
10. Total Cost

Out of the above 10 elements, three are injection moulded parts where principles of physics are applied.

Original costing

The original costing for these three injection moulded parts is given below.

Body	Injection Moulding	
	Pcs/Assembly	1.00
	Weight (kg)	0.05
	Material Cost	5.07
	Moulding	4.65
	Finishing	0.14
	Inspection	0.14
	Others	1.27
	Profit	0.35
	Unit Cost	11.27

Plate	Injection Moulding	
	Pcs /Assembly	1.00
	Weight (kg)	0.02
	Material Cost	1.50

	Moulding	3.65
	Finishing	0.04
	Inspection	0.04
	Others	0.39
	Profit	0.21
	Unit Cost	6.85

Cap Body	**Injection Moulding**	
	Pcs /Assembly	1.00
	Weight (kg)	0.02
	Material Cost	1.88
	Moulding	4.41
	Finishing	0.06
	Inspection	0.06
	Others	0.38
	Profit	0.22
	Unit Cost	7.81

Based on 12 persons (paid at Rs 8,500 a month) doing 1,000 pieces in 12 hours, assembly line running 24 hours to fulfill customer requirement, the cost per assembly is computed below.

Manpower needed = 24 per month

Cost of manpower: 24 × Rs 8,500 = Rs 2,04,000 per month

Assuming 30 days per month, the output is 2 × 30 × 1,000 = 60,000 pieces per month

The cost per assembly is Rs 3.4 per piece.

Taking the other part cost (in Rs.) to be fixed as below:

Spindle	1.8
Foam-57	1.8
Spring	3.6
Hex Nut	0.6
Packaging Cost	3

the total cost (in Rs.) as approved by the customer turns out to be:

	Body	11.27
	Plate	6.85
	Cap Body	7.81
	Spindle	1.8
	Foam-57	1.8
	Spring	3.6
	Hex Nut	0.6
	Packaging Cost	3
	Assembly	3.4
	Total Cost	**40.13**

The profit margin thus is 1.94%.

New costing

After the application of the principles, the new costing for the plastic parts is as below:

Body	**Injection Moulding**	
	Pcs/Assembly	1.00
	Weight (Kgs)	0.05
	Material Cost	5.07
	Moulding	4.49
	Finishing	0.14
	Inspection	0.14
	Others	1.27
	Profit	0.51
	Unit Cost	11.11

Plate	Injection Moulding	
	Pcs /Assembly	1.00
	Weight (Kgs)	0.02
	Material Cost	1.50
	Moulding	3.25
	Finishing	0.04
	Inspection	0.04
	Others	0.39
	Profit	0.61
	Unit Cost	6.85

Cap Body	Injection Moulding	
	Pcs /Assembly	1.00
	Weight (Kgs)	0.02
	Material Cost	1.88
	Moulding	4.13
	Finishing	0.06
	Inspection	0.06
	Others	0.38
	Profit	0.50
	Unit Cost	7.53

Now, if we add with these changes, the new costing (in Rs.) is:

Body	11.11
Plate	6.85
Cap Body	7.53
Spindle	1.8
Foam-57	1.8
Spring	3.6
Hex Nut	0.6
Packaging Cost	3
Assembly	3.4
Total Cost	**39.69**

This is indicative of drop in the manufacturing price. In terms of number, the cost fall is Rs 0.44 or 1.09%.

Innovating to optimize

For any innovation to take place, two factors are important.

1. The Problem
2. A vision/mind which is looking to cure the problem.

The problem

The customer's requirement was high and production line was unable to meet it without increasing the manpower (thus incurring an additional cost).

Analyze for finding bottleneck

Study the assembly line. To do time check, study on each station, find the problem point and give a solution.

Bottleneck identification

The bottleneck was identified at the station taking maximum time i.e. where screwing of bolts in the assembly was taking place.

Solution to the bottleneck

The present solution, in general, relates to an automatic screwing/ bolting machine. In particular, the invention relates to a foot-operated automatic screwing machine, which can be controlled pneumatically.

Elements of the solution

The principal object of the present solution is to automate the screw-fastening work by providing an automatic screw-fastening machine using a simple pneumatic control method.

Another object of the present innovation is to improve work/ production efficiency and safety of the workers.

Yet another object of the present innovation is to provide an automatic screw-fastening machine which can fasten screws of different diameters.

Still another object of the present innovation is to provide an automatic screwing machine suitable for the pipeline to overcome the prior art deficiencies.

Summary of the solution

The present solution provides an automatic screw-fastening machine to automate the screw-fastening work. The machine is connected to the conveyer belt for loading and unloading of the components. The screw-fastening machine of the present solution can effectively fasten screws of different diameters.

In a preferred embodiment of the present solution, the screw-fastening machine comprises a turn table which is provided with a pneumatic cylinder mechanism and a foot pedal connected to a motor and a pneumatic control valve.

In another embodiment of the present solution, the component to be screwed is placed on the turn table and the operation of the machine and pneumatic cylinder is controlled by a foot pedal and a pneumatic valve.

In yet another embodiment of the present solution, the product is placed at the table and the screw is placed at the designated position on the turn table which is attached to a motor. Once the operator places the product to be screwed on the table, he then presses the foot paddle to rotate the screw.

In still another embodiment of the present solution, the diameter of the plate in the table through which the diameter of the screw is fixed can be varied according to the need by changing the plates of different diameters.

Description of preferred embodiments

Accordingly, the present solution provides a screw-fastening machine that allows efficient mounting and advancing of screws carried on a turn table. The screw-fastening machine of the present invention essentially comprises a turn table which is provided with a pneumatic cylinder mechanism and a foot pedal connected to a motor and a pneumatic control valve. The machine is connected to the conveyer belt for loading and unloading of the components. The product is placed in a fixture place at the table (at a comfortable height for the machine operator) and the screw is placed at the designated position on the table. The location at which the screw is placed is essentially a turn table which is attached to a motor. First, the operator places the product to be screwed on the table, and then presses the foot paddle to rotate the screw. Once the screwing is done, the operator releases the foot paddle. The machine moves the screw strip forward to precisely set the screws at a desired positioning in a completely fixed condition. The device also comprises a holding means for stably holding the screw to prevent improper orientation of the screw and incorrect screwing, thereby, effectively and precisely screwing the screw to the target object. The diameter of the plate in the table through which the diameter of the screw is fixed may be varied according to the need by changing the plates of different diameters.

Numerous modifications and adaptations of the system of the present solution will be apparent to those skilled in the art, and thus it is intended by the appended claims to cover all such modifications and adaptations which fall within the true spirit and scope of this solution.

The creation of automatic screw fastening/bolting machine

The present solution provides an automatic screw fastening/ bolting machine comprising a turn table which is provided with a pneumatic cylinder mechanism and a foot pedal connected to a motor and a pneumatic control valve. The component to be screwed is placed on the turn table and the operation of the machine and the pneumatic cylinder is controlled by a foot pedal and pneumatic valve. The diameter of the plate in the table through which the diameter of the screw is fixed can be varied according to the need by changing the plates of different diameter. Hence the machine can fasten screws of different diameter.

The drawing of the machine

It is to be noted, however, that the appended drawing illustrates only typical embodiments of this solution and are therefore not to be considered for limiting its scope, for the invention may admit to other equally effective embodiments.

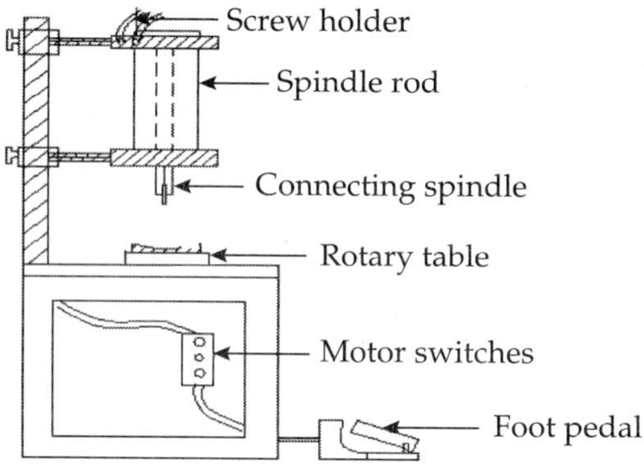

A Perspective View of a Screw Fastening Device

Concluding results

As this work is targeted towards the manufacturing industry and to show how we can improve the bottom lines or the profit margins, we have presented below live references to see the impact. As SPC was to study the impact, it will not be visible in the costing shown below.

Case Study: Ventilex 100

Request for Quotation (RFQ)

Plastic Mouldings – Injection Mouldings + Assembly

Now if we look back, then the cost of manpower in the assembly of 60,000 pieces per month will drop dramatically.

The number of people required on the assembly line now is 11 and the output increases to 2,400 pieces in 12 hours. Thus, the cost per assembly can be calculated as 60,000/2400 = 25 days.

Thus, only 11 persons are required instead of 24 earlier.

Manpower cost, thus, per month is 11 × Rs 8500 = Rs 93,500

Cost per assembly is 93,500/60,000 = Rs 1.56

Thus, after managing people and innovating the new cost (in Rs.) is:

Body	11.11
Plate	6.85
Cap Body	7.53
Spindle	1.8
Foam-57	1.8
Spring	3.6

Table Contd...

Hex Nut	0.6
Packaging Cost	3
Assembly	1.56
Total Cost	**37.85**

Now, taking into account (1) best possible use of Systems like ISO, 5S, 3R, Lean Manufacturing etc., (2) best application of principles of Physics, (3) innovation, and (4) managing people, the new results are:

Original Cost	**Profit**
40.13	1.94%
After Principles	
39.69	4.08%
After MP and Innovation	
37.85	9.14%

There are bound to be other aspects but we have tried to put forward only a few.

7

MANUFACTURING TO SUCCESS THROUGH CONTINUOUS LEARNING: THE KUNSTOCOM CASE STUDY

Kunstocom
Giving shape to ideas

Abstract

The pressure on companies to constantly enhance performance is more than ever before due to globalization. Nevertheless, competition is the key that drives businesses to constantly realign themselves with the dynamics of change. The joint family system, prominently grounded in India, is still the driving force that contributes to the success of many Indian businesses.

Kunstocom is one such example of entrepreneurs in India which can be looked upon as a synonym of 'success.' This case study focuses on the challenges faced by Kunstocom and highlights how it turned the challenges into opportunities and milestones amidst bottlenecks. It had a remarkable journey of setting new milestones in design and development of products, from the concept to the completion stage. From this case study, the readers will know what needs to be done to maintain business in the manufacturing sector. It highlights how the family businesses and their entrepreneurial initiatives have contributed to India's economic growth.

Keywords: Entrepreneurship, Challenges, Skills, Technology

BACKGROUND

Given the rapid pace of globalisation, fast-depleting material resources, increasing competition among nations and the growing need to protect intellectual property, strengthening the knowledge base is an important issue. Kunstocom is one such manufacturing company which has emerged successfully on account of its emphasis on continuous learning. With the right set of policies along with uncompromising commitment towards elevating quality, keeping in mind the cost as well as the interest of the clients, Kunstocom is treading fast on the road to achieve its vision. This case study was intended to focus on the challenges faced by Kunstocom and highlights how it turned the challenges into opportunities and milestones amidst bottlenecks.

IMPORTANCE AND APPROACH

Objectives

The study aimed to:

1. To study the role of entrepreneurs in developing the Indian economy.
2. To study the challenges that Indian entrepreneurs face.
3. To study the challenges faced by Kunstocom India Ltd.
4. To study the measures adopted by Kunstocom in its journey to success.
5. To study how as entrepreneur Kunstocom can contribute towards skill development.

Significance of The Study

This study is significant since it aimed to highlight what needs to be done to maintain business in the manufacturing sector. It highlights how the family businesses and its entrepreneurial initiatives contribute to India's economic growth. Its findings as well as suggestions will be of much help to the Government of India while they are designing their programs for promoting technically rich talents to become entrepreneurs and thus contribute strongly in developing India.

Methodology

This study employed the descriptive and qualitative research design to facilitate researcher's description of the case of

Kunstocom. McLeod, S. (2008) stated that case studies are in-depth investigations of a single person, group, event or community. Typically data has been gathered from a variety of sources by using several different methods (e.g. observations and interviews) by visiting the company. The case study method often involves simply observing what happens to, or reconstructing 'the case history' of a single participant or group of individuals i.e. the idiographic approach. Case studies allow a researcher to investigate a topic in far more detail than might be possible if they were trying to deal with a large number of research participants.

THE COMPANY OVERVIEW

The AKC Group resting firmly on a sound financial base, started its activities in India in 1976. Since the last 39 years, the AKC Group has spearheaded a revolution in many areas like plastics, pharmaceuticals, education, finance, construction, publishing & IT. With a well-planned and farsighted strategy by Founder President Dr. Ashok K Chauhan, the group has built up an enviable reputation and carved a place of pride globally.

Beginning in 1979, Kunstocom has been a remarkable journey of setting new milestones in design and development of products from the concept to the completion stage. Inspiration from the family members no doubt laid down the basic foundation of Kunstocom, but one cannot deny the efforts of Dr Abhinav Chauhan, the Director and CEO of Kunstocom who was endowed with an open mind to unlearn and relearn the key aspects of business and had the willingness to exploit the change in the market scenario rather than resist it. He had the relentless drive along with the competency to visualize opportunities where others could see threat. Initially, the road was bumpy. In the beginning, the lack of technical knowhow made an onslaught on the hitherto dull business, but Dr Chauhan set the ball rolling for the production of molds. Being an M. Sc in Manufacturing and Management Information Systems, he spent hours observing the mechanism of production. It was his quest for innovation which gave wings to his mission to soar high in the corporate cosmos. Attitude and skills can be cultivated, but passion for innovation and creativity has to see the light of the day through strategy. Dr Chauhan had the vision and competency to translate innovation into practical reality by managing it systematically in a strategic manner.

Table 7.1 Group of Companies

AKC Data Systems (India) Pvt Ltd	**Hardware and Software development**
Bacfo Pharmaceuticals (India) Ltd	R&D, Herbal Health Care Products
Cincorp International Ltd	Manufacturer of pharma containers by Injection Blow moulding in clean room.
Cross Border Placements (P) Ltd	Recruitments and placements.
Crobols -Cross Border Legal Systems (P) Ltd	Law Firm, International Consultants.
First Grade Force (P) Ltd	Security, Inteligents and Training Services
Krauter Health Care Ltd	Herbal Personal Care Products
Manz India (P) Ltd.	Production systems for photovoltaic-crystalline solar cell, CIGS thin film etc.
Stratega Finance Company Ltd	Financial Consultants, Merger & Acquisition, Strategic alliance.
Technicom Chemie (India) Ltd	Technology Transfer, Turnkey projects, Plant & Machinery
Tegro India (P) Ltd	Design, Consultant, Projects in real Estate.

The Kunstocom Journey

Kunstocom started its journey in 1979 and became a leading name in the world offering one-stop solution for designing, tool making and moulding of plastic components. The company boasts of the most advanced tool room and machineries. Kunstocom supplies over 4,00,000 aesthetic and fitment parts every day to major white goods and automotive companies. It is known for its quality, service and on-time delivery to the renowned OEMs in Europe, America, India and Asia Pacific Region. After extensive research and meticulous planning, Kunstocom started its Appliances Division with a promise to be efficient and cost effective. It is endowed with in-house expertise to give shape to any idea, to make moulds as small as 1 gram and as big as 5000 grams.

Table 7.2 Facts of Kunstocom

Kunstocom: Quick Facts
• Established in 1979, An AKC Group company .
• Core Competency include Design & Development of Mould, Manufacturing of Plastic Components for Automotive, Electronics, Consumer Durables and Assemblies
• Factory Area's of over 40,000 Sq. Mts. with Hi-tech plant, machinery and facilities
• ISO 9001, ISO/TS 16949-2009 & ISO 14001-2004 certified by DNV
• Stringent Quality Controls for incoming, in process finished products
• Statistical Process Control for consistent quality (SPC)
• Kunstocom products are the cumulative result of 38 years of engineering and plastic experience in GERMANY.
• Kunstocom is a customer centric company committed to supply 100% trouble free products with the best service back-up.

CHALLENGES OF KUNSTOCOM

Need to Redefine Family Business

Many bottlenecks were faced by Kunstocom. The family had to reorient itself in order to compete with the globally competitive environment and therefore, it was decided to diversify the business and move into the area of establishing the company in the manufacturing sector dealing with Design and development of molds manufacturing of Plastic components for automotive, electronics, consumer durables and Assemblies. It was realized that it was time to evolve and become institutional.

Choice of Machines and Equipments

The choice of machine, equipment and processes was a delicate problem which needed to be sorted. The size of production and the production process was large and hence needed undivided attention. Besides this, the availability of facilities of repairs and maintenance of molds, coolers, their spare parts was an immediate area of concern.

Skill Shortage

Availability of skilled manpower, which was professionally trained, was a critical area of concern for Kunstocom. Exploring the labour market and hiring the right fit was a major concern. These unskilled laborers had never undergone any kind of formal training and therefore were doomed to shift from one company to another on the basis of slightly higher wages and salaries. Therefore, the labour market was full of unemployed, less formally educated youth which lacked professional and vocational training despite work experience. Those educated, were found obsessed with text book knowledge where practical knowhow was absolutely missing. Hence the need for training was acute and incurred high expenses. Besides this, the attitude of the unskilled labor was not open towards learning. Therefore, much efforts were made to bring about a positive change in their attitude so that re-learning and unlearning may take place.

Inadequate Infrastructure

Though India has developed to a large extent, yet many parts of the country are still poorly connected by roads, railways and by power and telecom. The high transport and supply chain cost many a times posed a threat to Kunstocom. Raw Material is normally procured through companies which are primarily based far. Initially it was difficult to utilize the procured raw material into Kunstocom products but taking tough call along with production engineers, the company could execute the processes and arrive at the final products.

EFFICIENCY ENHANCERS

Readiness with Technological Automation

The manufacturing sector today requires a breath of automation. Technology has a high level of impact on businesses. Indian educational system is still lagging far behind in furnishing updated and current technological revolution to the students. An entrepreneur who is equipped with the latest technology can grow multiple times than an ordinary entrepreneur. The family inspired him to take on the decision and finally Dr Chauhan and his team of experts expedited the process of innovation by bringing in the latest engineering technology despite the rising cost, as in absence of trained manpower though the return period being long was feasible.

"In manufacturing, problems are faced at every step and everything in manufacturing revolves than its peers to grow in this industry. Today we have sound knowledge on every aspect of manufacturing. It is a hands on industry and you have to learn from grass root level, where you are expected to have top level knowledge or solution of a grass root level problem" - As said by CEO, Kunstocom.

"The company has embarked on providing one stop solution from conceptualizing to final delivery. Globally, this is one company which has the capability to execute a project from inception/plan to final product, which is the USP of Kunstocom. There is hardly any company in the world which does total execution of the project under one roof. Normally, it happens that somebody does the design, someone else does the mould, some other company does the finishing work, and finally the product is packed and delivered."- CEO, Kunstocom.

Process Floor in Kunstocom

Table 7.3 Processes at Kunstocom

Plastic Moulding
56 Nos. Injection Molding machines from 90 to 1000 Tons (1 gram to 5000 grams)
Backed with all ancillary equipmentse.g Chiller, HTC etc.

Diverse experience in molding – Engineering as well as " Difficult to run" polymers.

Polymers Processed

ABS and SAN ———- INEOS

Delrin – (POM) ——— DuPont

Polycarbonate; With or without glass filling ———- Bayer, Mitsubishi

High Impact Polystyrene ——— LG Polymers, BASF, Supreme Petro

Nylon (PA) – 6,66,11,12,46 ; With or without glass filling —– DuPont/DSM

Poly propylene with Glass, Talc or Mineral—– NPK Korea & Asahi Thermofil UK

LNP material —- SABIC

PPS material —- SOLVAY

Table 7.4 Precision Engineering

Design	Manufacturing
6 Seats	1 Seat
CAD/CAM/CAE	MOLDFLOW
UNIGRAPHICS NX-5 **PRO-E**	Flow, Cool, Warp, Shrink, Gas, Optim

Reverse Engineering Process

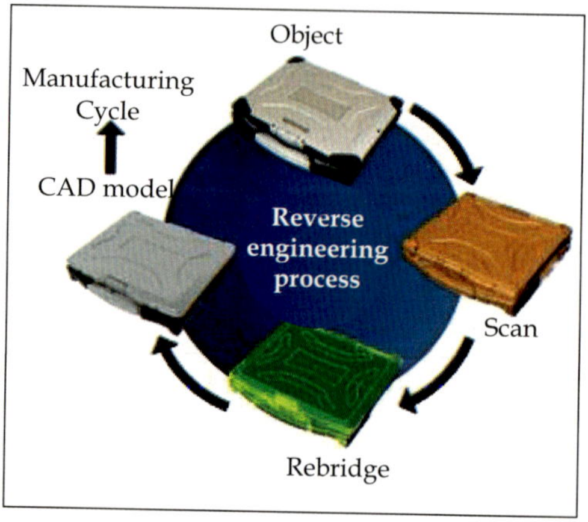

Table 7.5 Capability Mold Size

Max Mold Size	**1200 × 1000 × 450 mm**
Max Inserts weight on CNC	1800kgs.
Max Mold weight	7 Ton
Mold for Machine Tonnage	Up to 800 T

A plastic moulding machine

Table 7.6 Type of Molds

- Prototype mold
- Cold runner mould- two plate, three plate
- Hot runner mold & Hot Sprue mold
- External & Internal under-cut mold
- Hot sprue + cold runner mold
- Family mold
- Split & Stack mold Internal under-cut mold

The Post Molding Operations comprised Ultrasonic Welding, Screen Painting, Paint shop and Assembly.

Assembling a Complete Product

Raw material is normally procured through companies which are based at far and distant places. Initially it was difficult to utilize the procured raw material into Kunstocom products, but a tough call was taken along with the production engineers, and the companies started executing the processes and arrive at the final products.

No plastic remains the same once it goes through the molding process. Plastic shrinkage factor in microns is majorly considered while defining the quality of product. Lack of knowledge and willingness to learn made the company to finish the finest products.

Managing Unpredictability of the Fluctuating Demands of the Clients

The key determinant to success is to assess accurately the hidden or the latent needs of the customers. Thames (2012) observed, "Entrepreneurial attention is focused mainly on customer values". The Managing Director Mr. Anand Chauhan emphasized that Kunstocom was committed towards "Total Customer Satisfaction and prevention of Environmental Hazardous activity through continual improvement in product." CEO, Kunstocom states,"There have been several difficulties while interacting with the clients, because one needs to understand the client's pressures. For instance, one of the major clients of Kunstocom is LG. They wish Kunstocom to comply with certain specifications in order to retain their position in the market." Hence, the team of experts at Kunstocom tailors their products as per the needs of the clients which differentiate them from the rest.

People Management

An entrepreneur needs to master the art of people management. The CEO states, "Kunstocom has Technocratic work culture with a shade of Entrepreneurial Vision. The operational part is technocrat while prefix and suffix is entrepreneurial." Cross functional business processes are established at Kunstocom. Every vertical has a Divisional Head and the structural teams work in total tandem and integration with each other. The CEO knows most of their employees by their first name and also knows the problems of each employ. The CEO himself interacts with all team members, their families and kids. On the other hand, the company expects each one of its employ to give his optimum performance. The best part is that the DGM and above in teams act as catalysts and take a stand for the betterment of all.

The Human Resource initiatives are directed towards generating awareness, train and motivate employees for achieving individual quality and environment obligations through team spirit. The CEO states, "Today, we are one of the leading company in the world offering one-stop-solution for Design, Mold manufacturing and Molding of plastic components, with an impressive clientele present across the globe. We are better recognized as a team of experts who care for quality, service and on time delivery to the renowned OEM's in Europe, America, India and Pacific region". To achieve the goal, the managers strive for integrating improvement program for quality and environment in their performance. The effort is directed towards ensuring compliance with all the applicable legislations and regulations.

The in-house idea generation is given high priority. The team members from different departments are encouraged to share their suggestions across, due to which Kunstocom could achieve 20 patents filed in its name apart from the recognition that it received from National and International Bodies, which are summarized below:

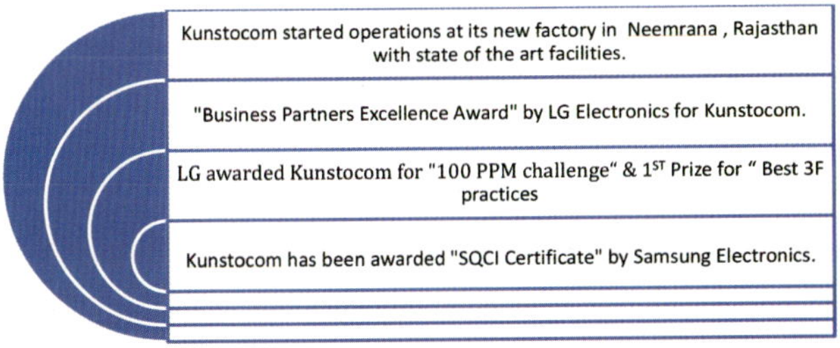

In today's dynamic competitive environment, the key strategic task of a manager is to reconfigure roles and relationships amongst a constellation of players ranging from clients to the customers. Hence, the company's paramount concern has always been to provide result oriented answers to customer's specific needs. This has been achieved through continuous reconfiguration and integration of the competencies and identifying the latent needs of the customers which were not identified by the competitors of Kunstocom.

Process Certifications

Processes are dynamic in a manufacturing company, and systems undergo changes very frequently. Today all the systems of operation in the company are certified by DNV under 14001 certification programs. In 1991, the company went for ISO-9001 certification. As the company entered in automotive business, the ISO-9001 certification was not accepted and hence in 2001 the company went for QS-9000 certification. However in 2004, the automotive industry said "we do not want anything other than TS-16949 certification." So the company obtained this certification. In parallel with the implementation of environmental laws, the country saw a huge hue and cry as what the industry is doing on Environmental protection. So the company had to again go for ISO-14001 certification in the same year. In 2011, the company entered in the appliances business where TS-16949 was not valid so the company went back to 1991 certification of ISO-9001.

The Growth Curve of Kunstocom

	1979	2014
No. of Injection Molding Machines	3	56
Employees	10	600
Plants	1	3

As it can be observed from the growth curve of Kunstocom, it had a very humble beginning with just one plant, ten employees and three machines growing up to 3 plants, 56 machines and 600 strong workforce, with growing business at national and international level. The company is processing about 24 tons of raw materials in various products, and has a product range from B2B and about 50 products under B2C category. The company has a decent size of marketing network which looks after B2C distribution.

CONCLUSION

Exploring the untapped Markets both at the National and International Level

Kunstocom plans to explore further the untapped National and International Markets. Low entry barriers have been there due to which the number of players have immensely increased in the domestic market. Owing to the presence of large number of players, coupled with low product differentiation, there has been an increase in the price wars amongst the domestic players. Therefore, the company today has emerged with distinct plans of going virtual in future, depending upon availability of resources. In this competitive era, going virtual is a tough call.

Presence in the Indian Market

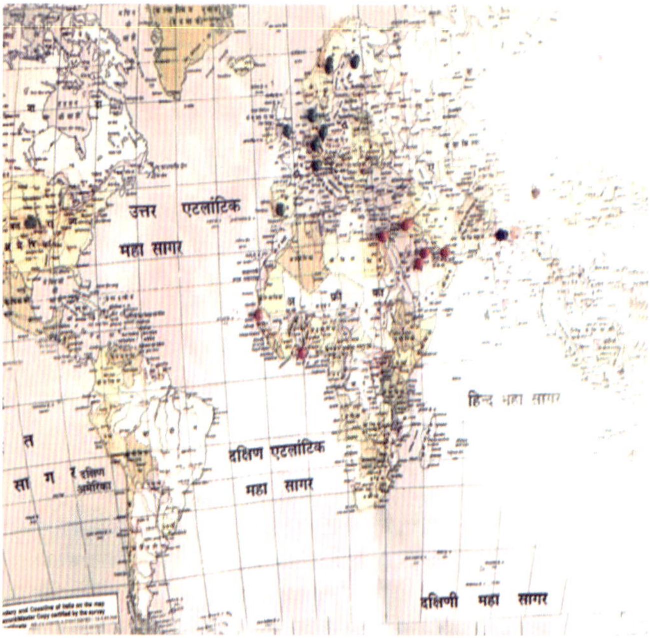

Presence in the International Markets

Promoting Skill Development

Maheshwari and Sahu (2013) emphasized in their study that, "India continues to be one of the fastest growing exporters of engineering goods, growing at a rate of 30.1%. The government has set a target of $110 billion by 2014 for total engineering exports". Business Today (2015) reports the Modi government has not only propelled the exports but has also hastened this process by convening conferences and seminars on the 'need for skill development' on the international platform. Kunstocom plans to have its own training colleges for the uneducated or less educated youth in different parts of the country where it intends to explore the untapped market and convert the raw talent into trained professionals.

REFERENCES

1. Thames, C. (2012). Peter Drucker's: Innovation and Entrepreneurship: Practice and Principles, http://knogimmicks.com/2012/10/28/peter-druckers-five-questions/ Viewed on May 3, 2015

2. Goel, A.K. and Farooque, A. (2014). Indian Entrepreneurship and the Challenges to India's Growth. TMIMT International Journal, Vol. 1, Issue 2, Dec. 2014, http://tmimtjournal.org/Pdf/Poceddings/Viewed on May 4, 2015.
3. GEM 2013 Global Report- Global Entrpreneurship Monitor (2013). www.gemconsortium.org/docs/download/3106. Viewed on May 4, 2015.
4. Jain, V.(2011). Indian Entrepreneurship and the Challenges to India's Growth. Ivey Business Journal,iveybusinessjournal.com/Viewed on May 4, 2015.
5. Maheshwari, D. and Sahu, S. (2013). Present Scenaio of Entrepreneurship in India. AISECT University Journal, Vol II, Issue IV
6. Kanchana, R.S., Divya, J.Y. and Beegom, A.A. (2013). Challenges Faced by New Entrepreneurs, International Journal of Current Research and academic Review, Vol. 1, No. 3, pp. 71-78.

APPENDIX

Independent t-test: The t-test is the most commonly used method to evaluate the differences in means between two groups. In this study, the t-test is used to test for a difference in opinion between two groups of organisations:

- HRIS Users and HRIS Non-Users
- SME and Large

In this study researcher has selected the significance level firstly at 0.01 and then at 0.05. The former one shows that the difference is highly significant and the latter one shows that it is significant.

The *t* distribution is similar to the normal distribution in appearance. Both distributions are bell shaped and symmetric. However, as compared to the normal distribution, the t distribution has more area in the tails and less in the center (Malhotra, 2010).

One way Analysis of Variance: The ANOVA is to understand, if there is any difference between groups on some variable. In this study researcher has conducted one way Analysis of Variance to examine the difference in opinion between the respondents of three groups of service providers. For example: Do the IT&ITES, Service and Manufacturing Sectors differ in terms of usage of HRIS? Is there any difference in opinion among the respondents of the three groups regarding the benefits of HRIS?

LSD Multiple Range Test: ANOVA examines whether there is a significant difference among the respondents or not, however, it do not specify, which group has the difference. LSD's Multiple Range Post-hoc Test examines this, and postulate, among which group there is exactly a significant difference.

Factor Analysis: It is primarily used for data reduction or structure detection. The purpose of data reduction is to remove redundant (highly correlated) variables from the data file. This study requires the factor analysis to reduce and classify the HRIS Advantages.

Regression Analysis: It is a statistical process for assessing the relationships among variables. It includes many techniques for modeling and analyzing several variables, when the focus is on the relationship between a dependent variable and one or more independent variables. More specifically, regression analysis helps one to understand how the typical value of the dependent variable changes when any one of the independent variables is changed, while the other independent variables are held fixed. The current study requires this technique to describe the extent of impact of HRIS subsystem on Strategic alignment of respective HR function.

Independent t-test: The t-test is the most commonly used method to evaluate the differences in means between two groups. In this study, the t-test is used to test for a difference in opinion between two groups of organisations:

- HRIS Users and HRIS Non-Users
- SME and Large

In this study researcher has selected the significance level firstly at 0.01 and then at 0.05.The former one shows that the difference is highly significant and the latter one shows that it is significant.

The *t* distribution is similar to the normal distribution in appearance. Both distributions are bell shaped and symmetric. However, as compared to the normal distribution, the t distribution has more area in the tails and less in the center,Malhotra (2010).

One way Analysis of Variance: The ANOVA is to understand, if there is any difference between groups on some variable. In this study researcher has conducted one way Analysis of Variance to examine the difference in opinion between the respondents of three groups of service providers. For example: Do the IT&ITES, Service and Manufacturing Sectors differ in terms of usage of HRIS? Is there any difference in opinion among the respondents of the three groups regarding the benefits of HRIS?

LSD Multiple Range Test: ANOVA examines whether there is a significant difference among the respondents or not, however, it do not specify, which group has the difference. LSD's Multiple Range Post-hoc Test examines this, and postulate, among which group there is exactly a significant difference.

Factor Analysis: It is primarily used for data reduction or structure detection. The purpose of data reduction is to remove redundant (highly correlated) variables from the data file. This study requires the factor analysis to reduce and classify the HRIS Advantages.

Regression Analysis: It is a statistical process for assessing the relationships among variables. It includes many techniques for modeling and analyzing several variables, when the focus is on the relationship between a dependent variable and one or more independent variables. More specifically, regression analysis helps one to understand how the typical value of the dependent variable changes when any one of the independent variables is changed, while the other independent variables are held fixed. The current study requires this technique to describe the extent of impact of HRIS subsystem on Strategic alignment of respective HR function.

BIBLIOGRAPHY

1. Beeman, Don R. Sharkey, Thomas W (1987), "The Use and Abuse of Corporate Politics", "Business Horizons" p26 vol. 30 issue 2.
2. Bertolino, A., Marchetti, E., Mirandola, R., Lombardi, G., Peciola, E. "Experience of Applying Statistical Control Techniques to the Function Test Phase of a Large Telecommunications System," IEE Proceedings – Software, V. 149, N. 4, August 2002, pp. 93-101
3. Burr, A., Owen, M., Statistical Methods for Software Quality. Thomson Publishing Company, 1996. ISBN 1-85032-171-X.
4. Carleton, A., "Statistical Process Control for Software (Software Technology Review)". Carnegie Mellon University, 2001. (URL: http://www.sei.cmu.edu/ str/descriptions/ spc_body.html).
5. CMMI Product Team, CMMISM for Systems Engineering, Software Engineering, and Integrated Product and Process Development (CMMISE/SW/IPPD, V1.1), Continuous Representation. Carnegie Mellon University, December 2001.
6. Card, "Statistical Process Control for Software?" IEEE Software, V. 11, No. 3, May 1994, pp. 95-97
7. De Lucia A., Pannella, A., Pompella, E., Stefanucci, S., "Empirical Analysis of Massive Maintenance Processes," Proceedings of the Sixth European Conference on Software Maintenance and Reengineering (CSMR'02), 2002
8. Deming, W.E., Out of the Crisis, First MIT Press, 2000. ISBN: 0-262-54115-7.
9. Farnum, N.R., Modern Statistical Quality Control and Improvement, Duxbury Press, Belmont, California, p.500, 1994.
10. Florac A.W., Park E.R., Carleton A.D. (d), Practical Software Measurement: Measuring for Process Management and Improvement (CMU/SEI-97-HB- 003). Software Engineering Institute, Carnegie Mellon University, April 1997.
11. Florac, A.W., Carleton A.D. (b), "Statistically Controlling the Software Process (The 99 SEI Software Engineering Symposium)", September 1999, Software Engineering Institute, Carnegie Mellon University.

12. Florac, A.W., Carleton A.D.(a), Measuring the Software Process: Statistical Process Control for Software Process Improvement. Pearson Education, 1999. ISBN 0-201-60444-2.
13. Florac, A.W., Carleton A.D., Barnard, J.R. (c), "Statistical Process Control: Analyzing a Space Shuttle Onboard Software Process". IEEE Software, July/August 2000, PP 97-106.
14. French, V. A. "Applying Software Engineering and Process Improvement to Legacy Defence System Maintenance: An Experience Report," Proceedings of the International Conference on Software Maintenance, 12-20 October 1995
15. Fisher,K. Self-DirectedWork Groups; McGraw-Hill: NewYork,NY, 1993.
16. Goodman, P.S.; Ravlin, E.; Schminke, M. Understanding groups in organizations. Research in Organizational Behavior; JAI Press: Greenwich, CT, 1987; Vol. 9, 121–173.
17. Goodman, P.S.; Ravlin, E.C.; Argote, L. Current thinking about groups, setting the stage for new ideas. Designing Effective Work Groups; Jossey Bass: San Francisco, 1986.
18. Hayes, W. , "Using a Personal Software Process to Improve Performance," Proceedings of the Fifth International Software Metrics Symposium, 20-21 November 1998
19. Humphrey, W., Managing the Software Process. Reading, Mass.: Addison-Wesley Publishing Company, 1989. ISBN 0-201-18095-2. 117
20. Information Technology – Software Process Assessment – Part 4: Guide to Performing Assessments (ISO/IEC 15504-4: 1998(E)).
21. ISO/IEC TR 15504-5 Information Technology – Software Process Assessment, 1998.
22. Jacob A. L., Pillai, S. K. ,"Statistical Process Control to Improve Coding and Code Review," IEEE Software, V. 20, No. 3, May/June 2003, pp. 50-55
23. Jaolte, P., Saxena, A., "Optimum Control Limits for Employing Statistical Process Control in Software Process". IEEE Transactions on Software Engineering, Vol: 28, No: 12, December 2002, PP 1126-1134.
24. Likert, R. New Patterns of Management; McGraw-Hill: New York, NY, 1961.

25. M. Brunett, C. Cook and G. Rothermel (2004), "End-user Software Engineering.", "Communications of ACM", p 53-58 vol. 47 issue 9.
26. McGregor, D. The Human Side of Enterprise; McGraw-Hill: New York, NY, 1960.
27. Montgomery, D.C., Introduction to Statistical Quality Control, 3rd Ed., J. Wiley, New York,P .677, 1996.
28. Montgomery, D.C., Introduction to Statistical Quality Control. John Wiley & Sons, Inc., Republic of Singapore, 1991. ISBN 0-471-51988-X.
29. Orsburn, J.D.; Moran, L.; Musselwhite, E.; Zenger, J.H. Self-Directed Work Teams: The New American Challenge; Business One Irwin: Homewood, IL, 1990.
30. Paulk, M. C., Chrissis, M. B., "The 2001 High Maturity Workshop, (CMU/SEI 2001-SR-014)". Carnegie Mellon University, January 2002.
31. Parker, G.M. Cross-Functional Teams; Jossey-Bass Publishers: San Francisco, CA, 1994.
32. Parker, G.M. Team Players and Teamwork: The New Competitive Business Strategy; Jossey-Bass: San Francisco, CA, 1990.
33. Paulk, M. C., Curtis, B., Chrissis, M. B., Weber, C. V. Capability Maturity Model for Software, Version 1.1 (CMU/SEI-93-TR-024, ADA 263403). Pittsburgh, PA: Software Engineering Institute, Carnegie Mellon University, 1993.
34. Radice, R., "Statistical Process Control for Software Projects". 10th Software Engineering Process Group Conference. Chicago, Illinois. March 1998.
35. Romine, J., "Using Statistical Techniques to Manage Software Projects with Data", SEPG 2002 Conference, February 18-21, 2002.
36. R.Y. Chang, A. Podgurski and J. yang (2007), "Finding what's not there: a new approach to revealing neglected conditions in software.", "Proc. ACM Int'l symp. Software Testing and Analysis", p 163-173.
37. Shen-Wen Cheng(2008),"Cost effective software architecture-based self-adaptation". Carnegie Mellon University.
38. Stevens, M.J.; Campion, M.A. The knowledge, skill, and ability requirements for teamwork implications for human resource management. J. Manage. 1994, 20 (2), 503–530.
39. Shewhart, W.A., Statistical Method: From the Viewpoint of Quality Control, Lancaster Press Inc., 1939.

40. Sutherland, J., Devor, R., Chang, T., Statistical Quality Design and Control. Prentice Hall Publishing Company, 1992. ISBN: 002329180X.
41. Weller, E. F., "Practical Applications of Statistical Process Control", IEEE Software, V. 17, no. 3, May/June 2000, pp. 48-55
42. Weller, E., "Practical Applications of Statistical Process Control". IEEE Software, May/June 2000, PP 48-55.
43. http://www.ibef.org/industry/manufacturing-sector-india.aspx accessed on 05/09/2015
44. http://www.cnbc.com/2015/07/14/apple-manufacturer-foxconn-to-build-12-factories-employ-1m-in-india.html accessed on 05/09/2015